CROSSING OVER and COMING HOME 2

An Analysis of LGBT and Non-Gay Near-Death Experiences

Liz Dale, Ph.D. and Kevin Williams

BALBOA.PRESS

A DIVISION OF HAY HOUSE

Balboa Press books may be ordered through booksellers or by contacting:

Balboa Press
A Division of Hay House
1663 Liberty Drive
Bloomington, IN 47403
www.balboapress.com
844-682-1282

Print information available on the last page.

ISBN: 979-8-7652-3109-8 (sc)
ISBN: 979-8-7652-3111-1 (hc)
ISBN: 979-8-7652-3110-4 (e)

Library of Congress Control Number: 2022912818

Balboa Press rev. date: 07/08/2022

Dedication

To my younger brother, Glenn Williams, whose queer identity has inspired me to appreciate LGBTQ+ issues and rights.

Dr. Kenneth Ring has made the following comment about this book: "I've known only a few gay men, but a fair number of lesbians or bisexual women, and I have long been furious about how gays have been treated, especially by religious authorities, in this country. So anything that would serve the cause for justice for gays, like Liz's book, would be my pleasure to support." Dr. Kenneth Ring also provided guidance concerning the statistical analysis of this project.

P.M.H. Atwater, L.H.D. has this to say, "Dr. Liz Dale has guts. She goes right to the heart of the Gay and LGBT movement and asks questions no one else does. Deep ones. She proved doing this that no one is exempt ... a near-death experience is a game changer. Doesn't matter preferences or druthers, life is wider, deeper, richer, sometimes even scary afterward. But real. Dr. Dale, you did it again. You helped us see our heart."

Contents

Acknowledgments

How can I express my thanks for all of this? There are no words to express my gratitude to the people who made this book possible. First and foremost is to Kevin Williams (www.near-death.com) who set the stage for all of this material to come together. He was able to get LGBT and Non-Gay NDErs to enter their stories and join in this project. How is it possible to thank all these NDErs for being willing to participate in this book project and share their amazing NDE journeys with all those who are interested in this deeply meaningful work. Our publishers, Balboa Press, are so very important and emersed themselves into this project to my satisfaction and to make this book possible for all to read.

I have to thank those who contributed to the first *Crossing Over and Coming Home* who shared their NDEs from LGBT prospectively. We now can easily expand to form a truly cross cultural look at NDEs from these two distinctly different groups. Everyone who reads this new book – *Crossing Over and Coming Home 2* – will see how important all of the NDE events/stories/issues are to all those who share their stories and to all those who read these accounts.

We believe that many more expansive studies will follow in which various groups/cultures/religions are all shared with the NDE community.

Cross Culturalism is an essential part of all our lives and looking deeply into various aspects of the NDEs that are available is one of the greatest gifts that we can share with each other. Read this book, send comments and suggestions for future studies in which various cultures can share their stories openly and with intention of being comfortable to share their amazing stories with each other.

Introduction

Both Kevin and I have been interested in the near-death experience (NDE) for many years. Kevin (webmaster of www.near-death.com) has been working with numerous NDE projects on display at his website and elsewhere. In this project he has been working intensively with me on the new project we call Crossing Over and Coming Home 2 over a number of years. The fact that cross cultural studies such as this one is the wave of the future is important to explaining current NDE philosophy and findings now and into the future.

My main interest in cross cultural projects started in 1996 at my first IANDS conference in which I came to realize that the LGBT NDE had not been looked at closely. Crossing Over and Coming Home began my intense interest in the importance for examining / collecting / reviewing LGBT NDEs. And now with the new Crossing Over and Coming Home 2 -- collaborating between Kevin Williams and myself -- we are able to publish these fantastic findings in which Gay (LGBT) and Non-Gay NDEs are compared and contrasted. The poster of 2022 which Kevin put together for the Salt Lake City conference is a 16 point Table of Contents / data from the areas we have been collecting. To realize the importance of these findings you can see our Survey Help Page / posted for the 2022

IANDS Conference following this explanatory introduction. My goal is to show examples of all #16 sections that make up this study. Please note that there are currently published here 41 NDErs who are non-Gay (62%) and 25 NDErs are LGBT (37%). From question 2 - 16 we examine responses to various interesting questions and specific NDE responses from both groups.

IANDS informed us today (5-18-2022) that Kevin and I have been accepted to put together a poster for the Salt Lake City conference which we will proudly display at the event.

NDE Group Definitions

Question #1 of our survey is for the surveyee to select the NDE group to which the surveyee belong: (1) LGBT Near-Death Experiencer, or (2) Non-Gay Near-Death Experiencer

LGBT is an acronym for a person's sexual orientation that stands for Lesbian, Gay, Bisexual, and Transgender. In use since the 1990s, the term is used to replace the term "Gay" because activists within the LGBT community believed that the term "Gay community" did not accurately represent all those to whom it referred. The acronym LGBT is intended to emphasize a diversity of sexuality and gender identity-based cultures. It may also be used to refer to anyone who is non-heterosexual who identify as Queer or are questioning their sexual identity. To recognize this inclusion, a popular variant of LGBT adds the letter Q, as in LGBTQ, which has been recorded since 1996.

Non-Gay is a term applied to a person having a sexual orientation other than homosexual; specifically, a person who is heterosexual. The earliest use of the term and its origin began in the 1970s as found in academic journal Current Anthropology according to the Oxford Dictionary.

Question #1 Statistics

Of the 66 NDErs surveyed:

41 NDErs are Non-Gay: 41 / 66 = 0.6212 = 62.1% of NDErs

25 NDErs are Gay: 25 / 66 = 0.3789 = 37.9% of NDErs

Conclusion: 62.1% of NDErs in the surveyee are Non-Gay. 37.9% of NDErs in the surveyee are Gay.

Sample NDEs

The following NDE testimony comes from a Gay NDEr concerning sexually diverse people: If this world was to ever find out just a small amount of what sexually diverse (gay) people are here to do on this planet, there would never be one single wisecrack or hurtful remark made ever again. Instead there would be great respect! People who speak disrespectful things about people of this orientation ... enact judgment, and do so from a place of unenlightenment, insecurity, ego and socially induced prejudice. Some may use mistranslated scriptures taught to them, not by the Holy Spirit ... but by fear-filled human beings. Many will choose to sustain a Divinely unsupported satanic hate-based rage against these children of God, rather than using Love to bring understanding and healing between both peoples. Christ said, the greatest commandment is that we are to love one another! When people sling condemnation, judgment and bitterness at others, they are not practicing the great commandment. They are allowing their Souls to fall into darkness.

When I got to Heaven, one of the first things I asked was about the very issue of bisexuality, as it had caused me a great deal of concern my whole life. My lady guide walked me to a room that had a large screen in it. On the screen, I saw two forms of Light conjoining with one another in the act of making Love. My guide then asked me to tell her which was the male and which was the female? I said, "I dunno!" She smiled at me and said it does not matter. She went on to say that the two Lights were what God saw when he looked upon us. She explained that God always sees us as our higher selves and that gender is a very temporary thing that will not be around forever. It was further explained to me that God himself is both a Mother essence and a Father essence to us, therefore; God fully understands our attractions for members of similar genders. It was told to me (or rather I was reminded) that there are no mistakes in the way each of us were made. God knew what each of us would be challenged and blessed with. We each act according to our heart (or developed Soul center) and as we mature Spiritually, we come up higher each time.

One other thing I was shown was a couple engaging in activities that focused on Lust rather than Love. My lady guide said that these individuals were in great spiritual duress and bringing upon themselves a life that would present much challenge. I saw that their Soul Lights began to dim significantly and there was a dark haze all about them. My lady guide then told me a time would come when these individuals would need to learn to come to God with their sexual selves, so that he could help them to use their sexuality in a more Loving way. More than likely, emotional or mental illness would emerge and help guide them to a more Loving path of expression. As I looked upon the figures, I sadly commented that lust was a major factor that involved many gay people. The lady smiled at me and explained that all fall into lust before we fully embrace the Light within ourselves. Later the lady also revealed to me that the two dimly beings in spiritual duress ... had been a married heterosexual couple.

The dark haze was what I call gray or shadow energy. This is a challenging type of essence that coexists with us on the planet. I believe this is what the Bible refers to as demons. These entities' job unto Creation is to help bring us additional weight and life obstacles which match our non-positive or unloving thoughts. With the weight of their essence on us, our inner Light is blocked. After a period of time where we go stumbling around in the darkness of our lives, we are once again encouraged to return to more Loving thought and action. As soon as we produce enough Light in our Soul from having been Loving, the gray or shadow energy is then popped off of us. Where there is light, darkness cannot remain! However, we must maintain Loving action and thinking because if we return to a less positive way of being, these entities return bringing reinforcements with them. When this happens it is time to do spiritual warfare!

Please never forget ... You are so Loved! Never is there a time where you are unseen or forgotten! To know Love ... you must practice Loving! Remember, your challenges in life are here as gifts ... once you succeed in getting past them, you will be rewarded by being filled with Loving and healing Light. There is no greater feeling than this. When in doubt, remember -- Love is always the answer! God bless you my precious brothers and sisters! Please know I am sending out Love and good energy to whomever will receive it! Be Loving to one another and Love will be good to you.

The following NDE testimony comes from a Gay NDEr: After I joined The Angels again, after my enjoying the books, I asked them was it okay for me being gay? I was assured "There was nothing wrong with being gay." Being gay or not, was like the difference between having blue eyes or brown.

The following NDE testimony comes from a Gay NDEr: She helped me slide onto the operating table and gave me a motherly look. "Don't worry. We know it's your first time. We'll make this a most pleasant experience for you." With those reassuring words, I drifted off to sleep. I awakened and found myself floating above my body, off to the right side, looking down, watching the attempts of the medical team trying to revive the lifeless form below. I viewed the scene with detachment. The surgical team was frantic. The color red was everywhere, splattered on their gowns, splattered on the floor, and a bright pool of a flowing red substance, in the now wide open abdominal cavity. At that moment, I didn't make the connection that the body being worked on was my own! It didn't matter anyway. I was in a state of floating freedom, experiencing no pain and having a great time. I wanted to shout to the distressed people below, "Hey, I'm okay. It's fantastic up here," but they were so intent on their work, I didn't want to interrupt their efforts.

I had traveled to another realm of total and absolute peace. With no physical body my movement was unencumbered. Thought was the avenue for travel. I floated up through blackness where there was no fear, no pain, no misunderstandings, but instead a sense of well-being. I was enveloped by total bliss in an atmosphere of unconditional love and acceptance. The darkness was warm and soft, a blanket of velvety love, stretching endlessly. The freedom of total peace was intensified beyond any ecstatic feeling I've ever felt on Earth. In the distance, a horizon of glorious white, golden light beckoned me forward.

As the brilliance increased and the encompassing rays stretched to meet me, I felt that time, as we know it, was nonexistent. Time and existence were a blending and a melding of the past, present and future into this one moment. A sense of all-knowing enveloped me. Every part of my being was satisfied with an unconditional love beyond description. All questions were answered. An inner peace without striving or achieving was created and understood.

It flashed in my mind; this was the pleasant experience the nurse had spoken about. I understood why she didn't elaborate. Words and descriptions somehow lost the essence of the experience. As I admired the beauty of the light, I was drawn closer, feeling the radiant warmth, infinite love and lasting peace. I felt as if I were home – home in the light. Before I became further engulfed in the light, I became aware of many spirits. They surrounded, embraced and supported my journey with their gentleness, knowledge and guidance. I felt one of them approach from my right upper side. This familiar presence came forward and my feelings changed to sheer joy when I discovered my thirty year old brother-in-law, the one who had died seven months earlier from cancer. My essence moved to meet his essence.

I couldn't see with my eyes or hear with my ears, yet I instinctively knew that it was "Wills." I heard his smile, saw his laughter and felt his humor. It didn't make sense, but it made complete sense. We were separate but we were also one. It was as if I had come home and my brother-in-law was here to greet me. I instantly thought how glad I was to be with him, because now I could make up for the last time I had seen him before his death. I felt sad and a bit guilty for not taking the time out of my busy schedule to have a heart-to-heart talk with him when he had asked me to. I realized I was not being judged by him but by myself. I was in his position – dying, wanting to say goodbye to those I loved, and then meeting people like myself not "getting it" – not getting that all the achievement, money or recognition in the world cannot be taken with you when you die. The only thing you take with you is the love you give away.

Wills gave love away his whole life. In a sense he was ready to leave our physical world and continue his work in the spiritual world. People, like my sister, who were left behind without their beloved, sometimes didn't understand. I would have to remember to tell Gwen about my discovery. The ones who depart are in a loving space with much guidance, understanding and purpose. Their wish upon departure is not to bring sorrow and grief to others but to honor the divine plan. It is their time for transition, for the continued development of their soul. Many times, the departed loved one will work in ways to help, serve and guide others.

Wills' gentle guidance allowed me to view my innocence. I understood, instantly, life was about people, not pursuits. I was putting pursuits first as a means to seek approval and love from people. Once I understood, I forgave myself for my actions and in the act of forgiving I received love in abundance. By giving love, one receives and experiences a tremendous love from the universe. Wills was like the "Spirit of Christmas Past." By reviewing my past, I was brought to new places of discovery within myself. Many events were shown simultaneously. I recalled two examples. When I was five years old I teased Tammy Fowler, another five year old girl, to the point of tears. I was now in a unique position to feel what Tammy felt. Her frustration, her tears, and her feelings of separateness were now my feelings. I felt a tremendous amount of compassion for this child. I was Tammy and needed love, nurturing and forgiveness. My essence gave love to both of us – a love so deep and tender, like the love between a mother and child. I realized by hurting another, I was only hurting myself. Again, I was experiencing oneness.

The next incident was similar. I had made fun of Billy Bradley, a scrawny, malnourished asthmatic kid. He died when he was seventeen years old from a cerebral aneurysm. He seemed to be in the realm of existence I was in. Yet, still I was not sure where I was. When Billy was twelve, he had written me a love letter that I rejected. I was experiencing his pain which became my pain. At the same time, I felt a tremendous amount of love for this boy and myself. My contact with him went beyond the physical and I felt his soul. He had a vibrant, bright light burning inside of him. Feeling his spirit's strength and vitality was an inconceivable moment especially knowing how much he physically suffered when he was alive. The message was clear. The message was – LOVE.

Above and beyond anything else, one must first learn to love oneself non-judgmentally and unconditionally. Then one will actually love all people and all things the same way. I realized how important people were in life, how important it was to accept them and love them. And I finally understood the old Mohegan Indian saying I had heard when I was in Girl Scouts, "Never judge another squaw until you have walked a mile in her moccasins." As I reviewed my life with Wills, my judgment prevailed and I remember thinking, "I've done worse things in my life." My question was answered before I finished my thought. All events in your life are significant. To bring an understanding of all things, even the experiences which you consider insignificant, will bring you to places of great awareness and compassion.

By the time my review was finished, I understood. I was aware of an almost cathartic release. I experienced emotion without the physical signs of tears. It brought me to a deep place of understanding and compassion. I never took the time to think how my actions affected others or how I treated myself. I felt a grieving for all my unconscious actions. With awareness of my unaware state, I released all the grief I had ever caused and joyfully moved into forgiveness. Other thoughts were conveyed and I remember thinking, "Wow, now I get it. Everything about our existence finally makes sense." I had more questions for Wills. The transference of information was immense and reassuring. He kept saying, "All is known. You have simply forgotten."

I didn't feel like I knew anything; yet, there was a place in me that knew everything. I asked Wills if I could stay. He said, "It's not your time yet. There's been a mistake. You have to go back." I remember thinking, "Okay, I'll go back, but I can get back up here." At that same instant his thoughts were mine, "You can't take your own life. Suicide, for you, isn't the answer. That won't do it. You have to go back and live your life's purpose."

I responded, "I understand, but I don't want to go back." Wills' thought came to me again, "It's okay. We're not going anywhere. We'll be here for you again." His last communication was, "Tell your sister, I'm fine." With those final thoughts, I felt myself going back, dropping downward through darkness. I was not afraid. Instantly, I felt myself slam into my body.

The following NDE testimony comes from a Gay NDEr: I felt my spirit leave through the top of my head. An angel accompanied me. I traveled through space, past the earth and the moon. Arrived at a different planet to study Goddess worship. The presence of god was all around. Full of love and peace. I was surrounded by others in spirit form. I visited many places and attended a concert in an amphitheater filled with the glow of amber. I returned to earth only to revisit many times. I discovered the Goddess. I fell in love with her and began to study her origins. My psychic abilities soared. Years later, I became a Spiritualist and a medium. I started my emotional healing journey.

The following NDE testimony comes from a Gay NDEr: In my NDE the first thing I noticed was that I was no longer in pain. Then I was surrounded in a Brilliant White Light almost unbearable to look at. An overwhelming feeling of a strong love I never knew on earth, filled me. A total non-judgmental acceptance for who I was filled me. I looked down at my feet, I was floating in white clouds, not touching any ground. "Weird," I thought. I looked up, seven Angles appeared around me. I was in the middle. They were all in brilliant white robes with hoods on. They had no faces. They were all very tall, about 8 or 10 feet. I began asking questions, as soon as I ask one, I immediately had the answer, as fast as lightning. I noticed my questions and their answers were by mental telepathy. We weren't speaking. I knew in my soul these were good Angels. Years later, I learned they also may have been my Spiritual Life Guides. They asked me what I liked most on earth. I said people and books. I was taken into an endlessly big room of books ... The last thing there (Heaven), was, I was asked, "Did I want to stay there with them or go back to earth?" I said stay there. But I was sent back because I was given a mission: to tell anyone who had lost a loved one about Heaven and my experience, to give them comfort.

The following NDE testimony comes from a Gay NDEr: During a brief amount of time, my spirit traveled through what I know and now call, "the Heavenly Realm." During the experience, all time stopped ... and two minutes of Earth time turned into what seemed to be days, weeks and even months. I saw an uncountable amount of wonderful places that were not of this world and many spiritual truths were Lovingly and generously revealed to me with mind-bending answers. Almost the whole time I was guided mostly by a being that appeared in the form of the most beautiful woman I have ever seen. Following us were three other guides who all appeared as men. All were robed with a beautiful glistening white, diamond-like material. I could also distinguish that they had Light coming from underneath their garments. I knew that this Light was their true bodies. The moment they came into my awareness, I recognized these beings as having been some of my closest friends that have been with me for all time. They were very kind to me and very caring about my feelings. There are no secrets in Heaven, so information that might have been considered embarrassing was treated with tremendous sensitivity. And even in moments where I might have cried knowing that someone knew my deepest darkest secrets, wonderful warm laughter was often exchanged between us instead. No matter any unpleasantness they may have known about me, I knew that I was eternally and unconditionally Loved! For many years, after my experience, I have continued to stay in contact with these dear ones through dreams and meditations. During my experience it was revealed to me that they had made many appearances to me during my life, particularly during difficult times in my childhood and adolescence, only I was not consciously aware of them or their presence at the time.

At first, I did not see God immediately. However, I did FEEL the presence of God everywhere! When I found myself in the Realm, initially I spoke with my very Loving guides, absorbed amazing information and took in the bigness of everything that was shown to me in God's Heaven. Then, toward the end of my experience, I stood in the wonderful presence of a great Being of brightness and knew with my whole heart that I was in the midst of my Creator, who is a being of unconditional Love and infinite Light. Many of you will not yet remember, but you too have stood in the very presence of God! I saw that before each of us are sent forth into our various missions, we are brought into a vast Cathedral of Light known as, "the Throne Room of God." In this room resides the very essence of all Creation, the Being those of us who are Jewish or Christian know and call Father God. This Being is the author of all that exists and he is tremendously pleased with all that has come forth from his Light. Because our Souls are covered by what is known as a "veil of forgetfulness," we are made to seek God out in ways that hopefully has us seeking him in each other. Each of us carries the Light of the Creator within us and it is through this experience we call "life in a flesh" that helps us to better understand the Creator and develop the inner Light he placed within us by practicing Love. A time will come soon enough where we will be back in the Loving arms of God and it will be a very Joyous time for us all. But first we must work at accomplishing the thing he sent us here to learn ... LOVE!

When I arrived in Heaven (in my experience) I found myself in a huge room where the walls and ceilings were made of pure crystal and they had Light coming from the inside of them. The effect was amazing. Then as I looked up, I saw four translucent screens appear (and form a kind of gigantic box around me). It was through this method that I was shown my life review. (Or rather I should say my LIVES IN REVIEW!) Without ever having to turn my head, I saw my past, my present, my future and there was even a screen that displayed a tremendous amount of scientific data, numbers and universal codes. I saw the beginning of my known existence as a Soul and saw that I had existed Spiritually long before this incarnation ... I undeniably saw that I had lived an innumerable amount of lives. Yet, what I saw went way beyond our comprehension of what we think reincarnation is. So, I am not exactly speaking of being born again and again on this planet alone. I saw that it is a big Universe out there and God has it all organized perfectly. Each of us is sent where we can obtain the best growth according to our Divine purpose.

Before the review ended, I was shown something that blows my mind every time I think about it. I observed myself go before what I understood to be as the Throne of Heaven. This is a great domed hall in the center of a golden city and is where the highest presence of God exists. What I saw was nothing short of spectacular! As I entered the room, I was washed with a brilliant white, golden and rose colored Light which filled me with indescribable happiness. I knew this Light had created me, as it had everything else. The Light was God ... both Father and Mother Creator mixed together in a colorful body of Light I have since learned to call, Christ.

As I looked up, the Light went on and on without end. I was lifted high up into the Great Light, and as this happened, I felt fully embraced by my Creator. I knew without a doubt that this omnipresent being found great delight in me and I clearly heard thoughts that I was considered a perfect being of the Creator's Creation.

I was told many things. But one thing has always stuck out in my mind: each of us have pre-planned moments where what I call, "clue events" will occur. These moments always trigger a memory that Heaven planted deep in the subconscious mind before we came here ... and once set off, the memory makes its way up to the more conscious part of our brain and enters our main stream of thought. This event then evokes a future thought or feeling in us, which sooner or later produces an action that gets us walking in the direction toward our destiny. If you understand the concept of "déja vu" you know what I am talking about. In Heaven, I saw over and over again, things that we see almost on a daily basis, which might even seem mundane ... could actually be clues for us to pick up on to get us going in the right direction! I understood that before we came to Earth, many of these clues were shown and explained to us and in our spirit we hold a deep knowing of what any particular clue really means for us. I saw that the conscious mind does not need to recognize a clue, (although Spiritually sensitive people will eventually begin to discern them), it is the eternal "subconscious" part of the mind that does all the spiritual work for us. A clue can come in the form of us looking at a clock at just the right moment and seeing a set of numbers that mean something to us ... it can be hearing someone say a familiar phrase or "trigger word" at a very interesting period of your life ... or it can be something as simple as seeing a single item sitting somewhere odd that intrigues you to wonder ... "Why is that thing there?"

I was then shown the time we call the beginning of Creation. There was a huge explosion, coming from a singing, pulsing, Joy-filled ball of bright Golden Light. I knew that I had been a part of this great Light, as have the rest of us. From this Light exploding, I found myself happily and quite excitedly hurling through space and time. I arrived safely in a perfect place of peace and amazing splendor. I knew immediately that this place was geared toward the expansion and education of every Soul that came there. I call this place, "the Realm." In this place, we are assisted by many wise beings and helped to complete many years of training and Soulish expansion. Where is the heavenly realm? In all honesty, the Realm is all around us, and not just above ... but directly in front of us. It is hard to see, but it is there. Heaven exists in another dimension that can only be entered by the way of Spirit. There are many different Heavens and Realms of Heaven. They are stacked one atop the other like pancakes and scattered all throughout God's super Universe. Each sits at a level that can accommodate those who walk within it. At the highest level is the Master Creator, God, and at the lower levels are the various forms and presence(s) of God. Everything is regulated by vibration, current and frequency ... the higher our spirit's level of vibration and frequency, the higher our Spirits are able to go throughout the Divine Realm. God, the Creator, vibrates at an absolute level that is so fast that he is perfectly still. His frequency is incomprehensible and is ever-expanding upward in pitch.

What does heaven look like? Glorious. There are many levels and dimensions in the Realm. There are great cities very similar to the ones we live in now, only these places have great harmony and balance to them. I saw whole cities made of gold and precious stones. One city that always stays in the back of my mind is a great metropolis made entirely out of what looked to be sapphires. It glows with the most luminous blue and white Light. It reminds me of a white Christmas tree with beautiful blue glass balls. I had a knowing that this place was where Loving Christ-like communicators choose to gather and exchange thoughts. There is a tremendous amount of Love and Grace in Heaven. No matter where you go, the feeling of Love and Joy is everywhere. There is no other place you would rather be. The point to incarnating in a physical body is so that once we are done, we can then explore the many worlds and places of wonder within the Realm. However, each of us is allowed a sacred space there, (where we can make a home for our Soul), if we desire to.

2

CHANGES IN BELIEF

Question #2 of our survey is for the surveyee to answer "yes" or "no" to the question of "Were there any changes in your values /attitudes / beliefs since your NDE other than religious/spiritual or afterlife beliefs?"

Such changes have been documented by Dr. Bruce Greyson and Dr. Kenneth Ring who jointly developed a "Life Changes Inventory - Revised" of "Psychological and Behavioral Aftereffects" of NDErs that includes changes in: (1) the appreciation for life; (2) self-acceptance; (3) concern for others; (4) concern for worldly achievement; (5) concern for social / planetary values; (6) quest for meaning / sense of purpose in life.

Question #2 Statistics

Of the 41 Non-Gay NDErs: 34 Answered "Yes"; 7 Answered "No"
Of the 25 Gay NDErs: 20 Answered "Yes"; 5 Answered "No"
Chi-Square = .0894309; p = 0.7649 > 0.05

Conclusion: Gay NDErs are not statistically more likely to have changes in their values /attitudes / beliefs since their NDE other than religious/ spiritual or afterlife beliefs than Non-Gay NDErs.

Sample NDEs

One NDEr (Gay) spoke of being a materialistic and selfish jerk who did not care about anyone or anything. After his NDE he spoke of changing into a "better person" by being more loving, forgiving, understanding, etc. He wrote of a goal to self-publish his NDE in the future.

One NDEr (Non-Gay) who described being in a duality of bliss - when he could go back to the NDE and became much more emotive (often crying). Now he has no fear of death. After his NDE, he became less patient in stressful situations and eventually had personality changes that led to he and his wife separating and ultimately divorcing after nearly 25 years of marriage.

Another Non-Gay NDEr wrote that after the NDE his depression and anxiety had decreased. He stated he is "actually glad to be alive." He was almost instantly in higher spirits and nowadays he rarely deals with depression. He went on to say, "I am a much more happy individual and my family have definitely noticed a difference ... It's been almost six years now and I can honestly say that I'm a much better and much more giving person after my NDE."

The following NDE testimony comes from a Gay NDEr: While I was in emergency, I became aware of my body floating upward toward the ceiling. I looked down, and saw a blond-headed physician working on me, and saw my mother sitting on a chair beside me, holding my hand. There was a medical tray beside my head and the doctor was taking things from there to help me. As I floated up, I thought: "Wow, this is really neat. I must be dying. This isn't so bad. Oh look, there's my mom. Aw, she must be so sad. Wow, this is something - look at the doctor. He might intubate me now. This is kind of interesting." I felt very light and comfortable, and not the least bit afraid. I was looking down, enjoying the experience, when

I thought: "Oh oh, if I die, then I won't see Maria anymore." Maria was my partner. All of a sudden, I was back in my body and unconscious. I woke up the next day in intensive care. Once I started talking, I described everything that happened in emergency to my mother, including the young doctor and what he did and said. My mother could not believe that I could do that, as I never saw that doctor again, and certainly never saw him when I was conscious. She thought I might be playing a trick on her. She had a lot of trouble accepting my story that I saw everything when I was floating up by the ceiling. I felt the whole experience was quite wondrous. It didn't challenge my beliefs. It wasn't scary. It wasn't even puzzling. It just was. I was grateful for the experience.

The following NDE testimony comes from a Non-Gay NDEr: In 1970, I had a profound encounter in which I was taken into the heart of creation, and back to the moment before the Big Bang. My NDE taught me everything that mattered: who we are, why we are here, and the nature of reality itself. To share and ponder this mystery is my greatest honor and joy. Somehow an unexpected peace descended upon me. I found myself floating on the ceiling over the bed looking down at my unconscious body. I barely had time to realize the glorious strangeness of the situation - that I was me but not in my body - when I was joined by a radiant being bathed in a shimmering white glow. Like myself, this being flew but had no wings. I felt a reverent awe when I turned to him; this was no ordinary angel or spirit, but he had been sent to deliver me. Such love and gentleness emanated from his being that I felt that I was in the presence of the Messiah. Whoever he was, his presence deepened my serenity and awakened a feeling of joy as I recognized my companion. Gently he took my hand and we flew right through the window. I felt no surprise at my ability to do this. In this wondrous presence, everything was as it should be.

Beneath us lay the beautiful Pacific Ocean ... But my attention was now directed upward, where there was a large opening leading to a circular path. Although it seemed to be deep and far to the end, a white light shone through and poured out into the gloom to the other side where the opening beckoned. It was the most brilliant light I had ever seen, although I didn't realize how much of its glory was veiled from the outside. The path was angled upward, obliquely, to the right. Now still hand in hand with the angel, I was led into the opening of the small, dark passageway. I then remember traveling a long distance upward toward the light. I believe that I was moving very fast, but this entire realm seemed to be outside of time. Finally, I reached my destination. It was only when I emerged from the other end that I realized that I was no longer accompanied by the being who had brought me there. But I wasn't alone. There, before me, was the living presence of the light. Within it I sensed an all-pervading intelligence, wisdom, compassion, love, and truth. There was neither form nor sex to this perfect being. It, which I shall in the future call he, in keeping without our commonly accepted syntax, contained everything, as white light contains all the colors of a rainbow when penetrating a prism. And deep within me came an instant and wondrous recognition: I, even I, was facing God.

I immediately lashed out at him with all the questions I had ever wondered about; all the injustices I had seen in the physical world. I don't know if I did this deliberately, but I discovered that God knows all your thoughts immediately and responds telepathically. My mind was naked; in fact, I became pure mind. The ethereal body which I had traveled in through the tunnel seemed to be no more; it was just my personal intelligence confronting that Universal Mind, which clothed itself in a glorious, living light that was more felt that seen, since no eye could absorb its splendor. I don't recall the exact content of our discussion; in the process of return, the insights that came so clearly and fully in Heaven were not brought back with me to Earth. I'm sure that I asked the question that had been plaguing me since childhood about the sufferings of my people. I do remember this: There was a reason for everything that happened, no matter how awful it appeared in the physical realm. And within myself, as I was given the answer, my own awakening mind now responded in the same manner: "Of course," I would think, "I already know that. How could I ever have forgotten!" Indeed, it appears that all that happens is for a purpose, and that purpose is already known to our eternal self.

In time the questions ceased, because I suddenly was filled with all the Being's wisdom. I was given more than just the answers to my questions; all knowledge unfolded to me, like the instant blossoming of an infinite number of flowers all at once. I was filled with God's knowledge, and in that precious aspect of his Beingness, I was one with him. But my journey of discovery was just beginning. Now I was treated to an extraordinary voyage through the universe. Instantly we traveled to the center of stars being born, supernovas exploding, and many other glorious celestial events for which I have no name. The impression I have now of this trip is that it felt like the universe is all one grand object woven from the same fabric. Space and time are illusions that hold us to our physical realm; out there all is present simultaneously. I was a passenger on a divine spaceship in which the Creator showed me the fullness and beauty of all of his Creation.

The last thing that I saw before all external vision ended was a glorious fire - the core and center of a marvelous star. Perhaps this was a symbol for the blessing that was now to come to me. Everything faded except for a richly full void in which That and I encompassed All that is. Here, I experienced, in ineffable magnificence, communion with the light being. Now I was filled with not just all knowledge, but also with all love. It was as if the light were poured in and through me. I was God's object of adoration; and from his/our love I drew life and joy beyond imagining. My being was transformed; my delusions, sins, and guilt were forgiven and purged without asking; and now I was love, primal being, and bliss. And, in some sense, I remain there, for Eternity. Such a union cannot be broken. It always was, is, and shall be. Suddenly, not knowing how or why, I returned to my broken body. But miraculously, I brought back the love and the joy. I was filled with an ecstasy beyond my wildest dreams. Here, in my body, the pain had all been removed. I was still enthralled by a boundless delight. For the next two months, I remained in this state, oblivious to any pain.

3

CHANGES IN PERSONALITY

Question #3 of our survey is for the surveyee to answer "yes" or "no" to the question of "Were there any changes in your personality since your NDE?"

According to this article on Wikipedia, "personality" is defined as: "... one's characteristic way of feeling, behaving and thinking which is often conceptualized as a person's standing on each "Big Five" personality trait (1) extraversion; (2) neuroticism; (3) openness to experience; (4) agreeableness; and (5) conscientiousness."

Potential sources of personality change include the impact of social roles on a person (e.g., employment), life stages (e.g., adolescence), and changes during old age. Stressful life events such as negative life experiences, long-term difficulties, and deteriorated life quality, all predict small but persistent increases in neuroticism. On the other hand, positive life events, and improved life quality, predict small but persistent decreases in neuroticism. There appears to be no point during the lifespan that neuroticism is unchanging over time. There are also multiple ways for an individual's personality to change. The Big Five personality traits are often used to measure change in personality.

According to Harvard professor Phillip L. Berman, there are ten major "personality changes" in people who've undergone an NDE: (1) an amazing ability to live in the present; (2) an abiding sense of deep confidence; (3) an immense decreased interest in material possessions; (4) spirituality becomes central and important; (5) a much higher natural compassion; (6) a strong sense of life's purpose; (7) the sense that all life and love has inherent value; (8) an amazing ability to enjoy a high degree of solitude and silence; (9) a desire to live a more social, communitarian, participatory form of life; (10) a strong sense of wonder and perennial sense of gratitude.

Question #3 Statistics

Of the 41 Non-Gay NDErs: 36 Answered "Yes"; 5 Answered "No"
Of the 25 Gay NDErs: 24 Answered "Yes"; 1 Answered "No"
Chi-Square = 1.26205; $p = 0.2613 > 0.05$
Conclusion: Gay NDErs are not statistically more likely to have changes in their personality since their NDE than Non-Gay NDErs.

Sample NDEs

One Gay NDEr responded this way: "To my absolute surprise and disbelief, I awoke at some point, and when I opened my eyes, it was as if nothing had happened, yet it changed every aspect of my life ... To this day, waking life feels less real than that experience - but in an extraordinarily positive way."

A Non-Gay NDEr responded this way: "I have watched countless NDE videos, read many books, and talked to others who have had similar experiences and have come up with this conclusion ... The years went by and I didn't discover anything until I read Dr. Raymond Moody's book, 'Life After Life.' Then I remembered that my drowning was my passage back into the light ... The search was over because I knew what I was looking for did not exist outside of me, but rather, within me ... in the silent space between my thoughts ..."

The following NDE comes from a Gay NDEr: I was a staunch atheist that thought religious and spiritual people were feeble-minded. I was so disconnected and disinterested in other people's life circumstances that I eventually disowned my entire family. [My NDE] happened to me while I was asleep. I found myself floating in an outer space setting, aware that I was pure consciousness without a physical body. I then saw the face of a little girl on a flat-screen TV monitor. She called me a bastard and the TV turned off. I then saw an arching tunnel of TV monitors that extended to infinity. They all suddenly and simultaneously turned on and I was instantly propelled through this tunnel. As I passed through each image, I realized they were (a) people I did not know, (b) from different races and genders, and (c) from various historical periods. With each image, I "felt" all of the pain and sadness they had experienced in their lives. Their feelings felt like needles pricking me and removing a piece of my very essence. Eventually, I arrived at the end of the tunnel where I saw a beautiful glowing sphere. And just as I thought this might be a sign that I was being "forgiven", I was thrust into the Eternal Void. It was so dark that it was actually devoid of color itself. I was made to feel as though I had been "deleted" from having ever existed, including life/reality as we know it. As I cried for "god" to help me, I suddenly sprang out of my bed and began running around my bedroom, screaming and bumping into furniture until I fell on the floor. The only thought that ran through my mind, over and over, was that I was so grateful to still be alive and not dead. I then tried my best to go back to bed as I had to get up and go to work in a few hours.

After the experience: Later that same day, after work, I received a telephone call from my closest cousin whom I had not spoken to in almost 3 years. She informed me that our grandmother had passed away during the night. It was the validation I somehow already knew, in my heart, that would explain what happened to me. My life forever changed 180 degrees and became a living hell for exactly 7 years, to the month. I lost everything. My long-term relationship of 10 years ended, so we sold our house and parted ways. I was fired from job, which ended my 10-year career in government. Consequently, I tried everything to escape my new reality. I became addicted to gambling at casinos, then it was sexual exploits, and eventually an unemployable alcoholic. During it all, I tried my very best to be a "better person" by being more loving, forgiving, understanding, etc. However, I remained skeptical and refused to accepted or process what had happened to me.

The day finally arrived when I attended my first IANDS meeting in Orange County, California. I was finally able to speak publicly of my experience without caring if people would judge me or think less of me. From that very day, my life has been a roller coaster ride of strange occurrences and phenomena to the degree that I felt compelled to write my memoir.

The following NDE testimony comes from a Non-Gay NDEr: I was a patient at Stanford University Hospital in 2005 for a Cardiac Alcohol Septal Ablation to help resolve a congenital heart defect diagnosed as Hypertropic Cardiomyopathy. The procedure went well, and I was back in Cardiac ICU with a temporary external pacemaker and leads through my neck to my heart. I was in good spirits, and my (then) wife and her sister left the room to get something to eat. I may have tried to use the bar above the bed to readjust my body in the bed. I was told that my heart stopped, probably because the pacing lead(s) became dislodged from contact with my heart. A Code Blue was called., and my wife had a premonition that the "Code" was for me and ran back with her sister to my room. The staff was in the process of administering a series of 6 attempts at cardioversion, but it only "caught" on the last one. At one point during the attempts, my wife recalled thinking/meditating, "You can do whatever you want, but you're going to need to do something soon."

When my heart started, I involuntarily inhaled gastric juices, and developed a high fever (106.4 sustained) due to Septecemia, Bactoremia, and Legionella for which I was packed in ice, and kept in a medical coma for 2 weeks. I developed DVTs in both lower legs.

My NDE experience was that I was suddenly in a hallway, rather pissed at why I was there, and what was going on. I saw a line of people moving to my left toward a bright light at the end of the hallway. I was almost immediately surrounded by several people who calmed me down and infused me with an amazing sense of love. A taller fellow came over, and told me that I was not expected just then, that I had fulfilled all that had been set out for me, and that it was my choice as to whether to stay or go back. I was thinking about that question, particularly about my youngest daughter, when it seemed I was suddenly back. I was angry because I had not finished thinking about the question. However, I recall thinking that whatever decision I made, needed to do it soon, almost the same words as my wife thought.

For about 6 months, I was in a duality of bliss - when I could mentally "go back" to that experience, and was much more emotive (often crying). Following that period, I found I had less patience in stressful situations, and evidently had personality changes that led to my wife separating and ultimately divorcing after nearly 25 years of marriage. I have had (and frequently continue to have) suicide ideation, and was hospitalized 3 times in Spring and Summer, 2009. I have no fear of death, and indeed, would welcome it. Ironically, I have had two more occasions to have died, but didn't really realize it at the time. One of those times was when I had cardiac arrest 5 times due to what was ultimately diagnosed as a failing pacemaker/ICD lead. The other was due to another bout of sepsis.

The following NDE testimony comes from a Gay NDEr: I was 12 years old. I was vacationing with my parents and two siblings in Mexico. We went snorkeling with a tourist group. I went out about 40 yards from the beach and had dived down pretty deep. I hit my knee against something sharp, possibly coral or a rock and gasped. I took in a lot of water and drowned before I could reach the surface. I remember drowning and how painful it was and how terrified I was. Once I passed out I felt as though I was in another realm. I had no physical form and could not physically feel anything but felt as though I had a new sense and felt very tranquil. A being, who identified herself as Eclipse, spoke to me. I was brought up Methodist but was rather agnostic myself. I knew there was nothing to prove, nor disprove, the existence of a god/gods or some sort of extraterrestrial being. Eclipse was a large cat of some kind with cone-shaped ears. She was matte black with short course hair and had green rings around her legs, ears, tail, and a ring centered on her head above her eyes. She and I spoke for what felt like an hour. She told me, "You are here now but do not have to stay here should you choose not to. You now have, and always will have, a choice to be where you want to be. Your meanings and reasons for going back or staying are your own and no one else's. There is no purpose you must fulfill that is not your own." I came to, puking my guts out, having pain all over my body. I felt like everything was dialed to ten. The smells, sounds, tastes, feeling, and sight of everything and everyone was overloading my mind. I had a lot of difficulty adjusting and I couldn't sleep for five days. I had a stroke when I drowned, something that apparently isn't that rare. It took about 6 months to be able to move much of my left side of my body which had been paralyzed. From the drowning and stroke, I suffer from depression, DID, OCD, ADHD, Ictal Headaches, Complex Partial Seizures, and have a very difficult time remembering basic things. I know my personality changed a lot. I used to be Extroverted, having always felt energized by being around people. I'm very much Introverted now.

4

CHANGES IN OUTLOOK ABOUT
LIFE AND DEATH

Question #4 of our survey is for the surveyee to answer "yes" or "no" to the question of "Were there any changes in your outlook about life and death since your NDE?"

There are changes in NDErs outlook about life and death according to the IANDS.org website: "The average near-death experiencer comes to regard him or herself as 'an immortal soul currently resident within a material form so lessons can be learned while sojourning in the earth plane.' They now know they are not their body... Eventually, the present life, the present body, becomes important and special again."

There are a number of important changes NDErs undergo according to a JNDS guest editorial by Craig Lundahl, Ph.D.: (1) losing their fear of death; (2) not taking life for granted because life is more precious and a wonderful gift; (3) every human being has a life purpose or mission; (4) having no doubt an afterlife exists; (5) believing suicide is not a good option; (6) learning that social position and wealth are not important; (7)

understanding that gaining knowledge and love are the most important things.

Question #4 Statistics

Of the 41 Non-Gay NDErs: 39 Answered "Yes"; 2 Answered "No"
Of the 25 Gay NDErs: 23 Answered "Yes"; 2 Answered "No"
Chi-Square = 0.265869; p = 0.6061 > 0.05
Conclusion: Gay NDErs are not statistically more likely to have any changes in their outlook about life and death since their NDE than Non-Gay NDErs.

Sample NDEs

In relation to every human being having a life purpose or mission, one Non-Gay NDEr wrote: "Death for me seemed factual with an order of logical progression and profound spirituality ... I learned all human beings are shrouded in ignorance, by design, in order to learn hard lessons through each life we live. When you die, the superficial facade falls away and we awaken from the dream into the truth."

A Gay NDEr wrote (in regards to not taking life for granted): "To this day, I am deeply compassionate to all people, animals, and nature. Trees fascinate me. Sometimes when I see flowers, I still start crying. They're so beautiful. Sometimes I attend funerals of people I don't know to tell them my experience ... I have experienced space and universal travel as I sleep. I have met former friends who have passed over years ago. I have been saved from certain bodily harm by my guides and angels several times.

The following NDE testimony comes from a Gay NDEr: As a child I was assaulted multiple times over and later developed a rare neuroligical disorder which was debilitating daily. The meds wouldn't work so I was told I could drink and drink I did. So by the time I was 25 I was a raging alcoholic, and in so much pain I was depressed and in a bad place. The night of my NDE I was attacked by dark entities for days until I could no longer continue and I cried out from the deepest part of me that I surrender. All stopped and went silent and peaceful. To start I realized I was in my body but I heart had stopped. I went through several amazing things and about 8 minutes later, my heart restarted and I was back in my body. A few minutes months later I had a massive seizure and stroke and an out of body. My life has been turned around 180. I have been cured of my rare disorder and my alcoholism. I couldn't be happier now. Its like I had a hell ish first chapter of my life and I am looking forward to the heavenly chapter that is next.

The following NDE testimony comes from a Non-Gay NDEr: Left body 4 times in life beginning at the age of 5. Each time either went to another beautiful land filled with glowing foliage and landscape always with others near or at a distance. Last one was confronted by a large man (an angel) who was a no nonsense determined I was going to hear and see what he had been ordered to show. I argued but eventually he won. It was graphically shown what would happen, in ripple effect, if I stayed dead. (Yes, I knew was out of my body. No pain.) Although I could see the beautiful land and a city in the distance, I was not allowed to go farther as heretofore for rest. There is still a struggle with honest "integration" to mortal life.

The following NDE testimony comes from a Non-Gay NDEr: I had a horse accident. Was in a coma for 13 days but I was wide awake inside my body and could not move. All medical people wanted me to die, thought I was brain dead. I died twice and was told by spirit it was not my time. I spoke to all my guides 15 - 20 of them. Whenever I had to much pain they would take me out of my body so I could get away. I am still able to jump out anytime. I was in the coma for 13 days, had a Trachea, lung tubes each side of my body, after I came out of the coma they put in a stomach tube, in the hospital for 21 days but went home with no rehab of any kind. Off work for 3 months and lead a normal life but with PTSD. You may contact me if you want at cspookyc@gmail.com

The following NDE testimony comes from a Non-Gay NDEr: I basically saw the meaning of life. I saw a body going into the heavens, It was so beautiful in the presence of this energy that I cried. I just couldn't take the overwhelming beauty.

The following NDE testimony comes from a Gay NDEr: I should be clear that my experience occurred after I took ayahuasca, a potent psychoeffective tea that is typically administered by shamans for spiritual and physical healing purposes. I have taken it a number of times for these purposes, in part because I live with an often-painful chronic illness. A few of the experiences included what might be said to be out-of-body or "otherworldly" events. The last time I took it went far beyond that. The ayahuasca was much more potent than it had been before, or affected me in a more potent way. I was overcome by visions, which I for some reason had never seen before, and that alarmed me, and then after a long struggle I was taken out of my body. I was certain that I had died, and I continued to bargain and battle to keep my life. I underwent a life review process during which I re-experienced many events or times of my life, including being in utero, traumatic and mundane events. Some of these felt as if they lasted for weeks; time was no longer linear and did not function as it does here. I was entirely detached from my body and the reality that I had died was undeniable, and I continued to bargain for the return to my body and my life, but was repeatedly told (by whom I don't know) that I had made a mistake and that mistake had had its consequence. It was terrifying primarily because I did not want to traumatize my family with my premature death, and because I knew that the story of my life was had not been lived to completion. I eventually accepted that this life had ended unexpectedly, and I was in a sort of holding place awaiting a new life. During the bargaining process, I alternately encountered an entirely overwhelming and disturbing amount of information, including thousands of colors, numbers and information that makes up the physical world. It was disturbing to see life in this objective form—everything and everyone was just that, and I was part of it and no longer an individual. It was overwhelming.

To my absolute surprise and disbelief, I awoke at some point, and when I opened my eyes it was as if nothing had happened—yet it changed every aspect of my life. I went to work as usual but I had to confess what had happened to a colleague so that I could ask if I was alive, because it felt like some sort of mirage. To this day, waking life feels less real than that experience—but in an extraordinarily positive way. The limits of the natural world are blissful—I feel shielded from the overwhelming amount of information that exists in the world through the filters of the senses. I have literally jumped up and down in appreciation of gravity. Relationships that once felt overwhelmingly arduous and complicated and tiring now feel very simple, very cut and dry. I now see human beings in many ways as I've always seen animals, which is neither good nor bad, just as creatures that act according to instinct and senses and intuition, and which in a great number of ways are naïve and innocent even when what we do seems otherwise to us. Life feels in a more real way than ever like a classroom and an adventure: a place to act according to conscience and to at the same time revel in perceptions and knowledge. As a young gay man, my default in any stressful situation was "if it gets bad enough, killing myself is a way out." As a result of my ayahuasca experiences and particularly the NDE, my default now is "you have to get through this to learn the lessons you.

The following NDE testimony comes from a Non-Gay NDEr: When I was 17 I was rushed to the hospital since I had been extremely sick for over a week and I finally collapsed. They ran some tests at the ER and the ER doctor said I would need immediate surgery to remove my appendix since it looked like I had appendicitis. I remember passing out while I was waiting for my surgeon to arrive and while I was passed out, I remember feeling like I was floating somewhere bright and sunny. I remember feeling an overwhelming sense of peace, tranquility and happiness. It's hard to put into words, but I felt like I was truly at peace with myself and I felt like I was one with the universe. Then suddenly I woke up in a hospital room all by myself and the first thing I did was cry my eyes out and at that moment I knew "God" / a higher power existed. Before this near-death experience, I had convinced myself that God and religion were a farce. I questioned everything I was taught as a kid at Sunday mass. Growing up I thought to myself "If god exists, why are there countless children being raped? Why are there countless people living in poverty or starving on a daily basis? Why are countless babies and children being diagnosed with cancer and other terrible diseases?" I was convinced the existence of God was ridiculous since a decent omnipotent being wouldn't let these types of things happen. After my NDE though, my outlook on life and God has changed drastically. I don't practice a specific religion but I truly believe in a higher power. I'm what people consider a "Deist". I'm thankful to be alive and I wouldn't be here if it wasn't for my surgeon, his staff, the doctors at the ER and I truly feel God played a role as well. Before my NDE i struggled with depression and anxiety and after my NDE I was actually glad to be alive, I was almost instantly in higher spirits and now a days I rarely deal with depression. I'm a much more happy individual and my family has definitely noticed a difference. It's been almost 6 years now and I can honestly say I'm a much better and much more giving person after my NDE.

5

CHANGES IN RELIGIOUS OR SPIRITUAL BELIEFS

Question #5 of our survey is for the surveyee to answer "yes" or "no" to the question of "Were there any changes in your religious or spiritual beliefs since your NDE?"

Dr. David San Filippo has pointed out how Dr. Kenneth Ring, in his book Heading Toward Omega: In Search of the Meaning of the Near-Death Experience (1985), documented how many NDEs act as a catalyst toward a spiritual awakening for the NDEr:

"What is noteworthy ... is the particular form this spiritual development takes in many NDErs - i.e., the real significance of the NDE here may not be simply that it promotes spiritual growth as much as the kind of spiritual growth it promotes" (p. 144). This awakening appears to move the experiencer toward what Ring (1985) calls a "universalistically spiritual orientation" (p. 145). He defines universalistically spiritual orientation as consisting of: (1) a tendency to characterize oneself as spiritual rather than religious, per se; (2) a feeling of being inwardly close to God; (3) a de-emphasis of the formal aspects of religious life and worship; (4) a conviction that there is life after death, regardless of religious belief; (5) an openness to the doctrine of reincarnation (and a general sympathy towards eastern religions); (6) a belief in the essential underlying unity of all religions; (7) a desire for a universal religion embracing all humanity (p. 146).

Question #5 Statistics

Of the 41 Non-Gay NDErs: 30 Answered "Yes"; 11 Answered "No"
Of the 25 Gay NDErs: 23 Answered "Yes"; 2 Answered "No"
Chi-Square = 3.48109; $p = 0.06207 > 0.05$
Conclusion: Gay NDErs are not statistically more likely to have any changes in their religious or spiritual beliefs since their NDE than non-gay NDErs.

Sample NDEs

One Non-Gay NDEr wrote: "For a split second I saw an image of a peaceful man in a blue turban and my impression was that there are many religions and one was no better than the other. I saw two profiles of faces, eye to eye, floating, looking into each others eyes and, at the same time, I 'heard' 'Tell others.' They wanted me to tell people what happened and what I had learned ... I was told when someone suffers at the end of their life, there is a reason and purpose, a sort of burning away of karma, although that word was never used. There would be a benefit to the other side.

A Gay NDEr wrote: "During my NDE, I learned the secrets of the universe but had to forget almost everything before being sent back to my body. In fact, he told me that I would only be able to remember what was important for humanity as a whole, and that is to love every other without judging. He said that humans judge; our Creator does not. I recall being amazed at space and star stuff, but that's all I remember about the universe ... just the being in awe."

The following NDE testimony comes from a Non-Gay NDEr: I have watched countless NDE videos, read many books, and talked to others who have had similar experiences and have come up with this conclusion ...

what I experienced / remembered is the absolute earth-truth for me. Remembering my Light-experience consists of a unique "knowing and feeling" that I have not experienced again in any other earth-event. In my concluding years here on planet earth, I am filled with a "peace and joy" that can only come from the "infinite, unconditional loving Light." My best analogy is that my life here on planet earth, in this particular three-dimensional space and linear time segment, is like a Broadway play. A play in which I am the lead character and for most of my earth-life I thought that this play was "reality." I forgot that it is just a play, a fiction created by me (Light-Andy) to experience the exhilaration of "knowing" after experiencing "not-knowing" for a long period of earth-time. I remember that in the Light there is no "NOT KNOWING." In order for Light-Andy to experience "not-knowing," Light-Andy had to choose to lower his vibration so that he could incarnate on a three-dimensional, linear time planet like earth.

And I did. I spent years searching for the answer to the question "What the hell really happened to me the day drowned?" I thought that the next book, the next religion, the next guru, the next "something" would tell me what happened to me when I drowned and why. The years went by and I didn't discover anything until I read Dr. Raymond Moody's book, "Life After Life." Then I remembered that my drowning was my passage back into the Light, and my return to planet earth was a choice to continue the earth-experience for a few more earth-years. The search was over because I knew what I was looking for did not exist outside of me, but rather, within me ... in the silent space between my thoughts. That is where the Light vibrates within me, within everything. The unconditional loving Light is all and everything there IS. And earth-Andy is one of the infinite, vibrating, holographic piece of the Light. Wow, it is so simple now! — My interpretation of reality comes solely from my "remembering." Once I remembered that I am a piece of the Light, I stopped looking for confirmation from the "outside."

Other NDErs have their own "remembering" and their memories may be different but, at the same time, they are all the same. I have nothing to sell, nothing to prove, nothing to apostatize ... I am here to share my remembrances with those who wish to listen and share their own memories with me. — The three most significant memories that I have about my NDE is that in the Light there is no hierarchy, no judgment, or no separation. Wow, once I remembered that those three concepts did not exist in the Light, everything else about the Light made sense to me. Earth-Andy remembered that we are truly ONE, and in order to be ONE with the universe ... hierarchy, judgment, and separation cannot exist. We are all composed of vibrating strings of energy; vibrating strings of unconditional Love; vibrating, holographic, strings of the Light. The different vibrating pieces of Light make us unique, but we are absorbed into ONE Light. The Light is truly very simple!

The following NDE testimony comes from a Gay NDEr: It is impossible for me to fully describe everything about my "near-death experience," but below is my attempt at the gist of it. At nineteen, I was in a near fatal auto accident. Geez, that word, fatal! It supposedly means causing ruin or destruction, but it taught me that there is no such thing as death. I learned in one swift moment that separation from the body means freedom for the spirit. I remember that I froze in position when I saw a car crossing the medium and heading for me. My arms locked on the steering wheel, and my left leg braced the floor of the car so hard that when the oncoming car hit, the impact caused my arms to snap (the ulna and humerus in both) as well as the foot and femur of my left leg. On impact, the other vehicle pushed me into what had been the backseat of my car. Something under the hood cut my right arm at the shoulder and in the armpit area, causing the arm to be cut so severely that it was barely attached. My pelvic bone was also broken. But as auto accidents go, I was lucky because I didn't suffer head injuries nor was I going to come out of this a paraplegic. However, I did "give up the ghost," so to speak.

I died before the Jaws of Life could get my body out of the car. I can still see the image of the nineteen-year-old bloody, lifeless, Sherry. My hair was long, and I was wearing a yellow button-up shirt and blue jeans. The body was upright and hunched over. My spirit was no longer inside that mass of flesh but hovering over it. The spirit me was very nervous, it (I) was still in earth's realm; in fact, it was still inside the car at this time, peering down at my face. The spirit me heard the me that was hunched over and bloody call out for my mother. I guess it was as I was in the process of dying. I whimpered, "Mama, Mama."

Then suddenly, my spirit was in, what I can only describe as, a different realm, and I was no longer afraid. Oh, I might add that I did not leave earth via a tunnel but did eventually return to my body through one. For years, I have searched for words to describe that realm, to no avail. In that place, I inhaled love, exhaled love, and floated in love; a love like we've never experienced here on earth. It isn't possible for it to exist here. I was told this, and many other things, by a man standing (floating) beside me. He didn't identify himself, but he let me know that he was a go-between (connecting link) for the Creator and me. It was revealed to me that who he was wasn't as important as his message. This "go-between" wore a long, white, Arabic-type thobe that had a around the waist. He wore nothing on his head, and his hair was thick, wavy, dark, and shoulder length. He was calm and reassuring as he "spoke," which was by means of telepathy— that's how we communicated with each other, and it seemed very natural. No need for vocal cords, yet I could hear myself, and I could hear him. It was as if the vocal cords were our minds.

During my NDE, I learned the secrets of the universe, but had to forget almost everything before being sent back to my body. In fact, he told me that I would only be able to remember what was important for humanity as a whole, and that is to love each other without judging. He said that humans judge, our Creator does not. I recall being amazed at space and star stuff, but that's all I remember about the universe, just the being in awe. Information I was able to retain after re-entering my body

(1) Earth is a school for our souls to grow, and how we respond to the suffering of others is an indicator of our level of soul growth. (2) Loving each other unconditionally, without judgment, and developing our compassion is what we are put on earth to do. And until we get to the point that we can

do these things, we will reincarnate (in other words, we will be born again). (3) We reap what we sow. No one escapes that. It's one way our souls grow. We will all feel the pain we've caused others and in the same manner. If it doesn't happen to us directly, we will witness it in our loved ones, but we will go through the experience — if not in this lifetime, a future one. (4) The "go-between" said that we are all connected at a soulular level and that just as we have our parents' DNA on earth, our souls are made of the same thing that our Creator is made of, but to a lesser degree. (5) He said that there are no "chosen ones" and that our Creator loves everyone equally, no matter what race, religion, or region. (6) He told me that man created religion and that death and destruction are what it brings. However, he said that spirituality is important. It's our soul's attempt to reach out to its Creator, to home. Spirituality is good; religion, however, is our attempt to reach out to God, not God's attempt to reach us. Our Creator is already, and always, with us.

While floating in this beautiful realm, I remember feeling sorry for the paramedics who were working on me and for the friend who was also in the accident. She wasn't hurt too badly, but I did see her crying at one point. They seemed to be worried for me, I was confused about that. I couldn't understand why they weren't happy for me. After all, I was (what felt like) home. I couldn't wait for my family to join me. There is no such thing as time there, so I had no concept of when they would be joining me, just that they would at some point, and that we would all be there together.

I knew that without a doubt. I could see the blood on the body that was now laying on the ground. I (the spirit me) stretched out my arms and saw no blood, no injuries at all. I said, "Here I am! Look at me." No one looked up. I was puzzled for a moment, as I could see and hear them—I could even feel their sadness—but they could not see or hear me. I began to feel sorry for them, for everyone on earth. They were trapped in hell and had no idea. It's a hell that we human beings create for ourselves, and sadly, for others because of our jealousies and prejudices.

I saw a police officer walk to his car. From there, he notified someone to call my mother to tell her I was dead. The second she got the news, a window box opened up and I could see her reaction. She started crying and saying, "Oh God, no!" At that moment, I knew that, because of her prayers and tears, I was going to have to go back into the broken body. I pleaded with the man who had been with me in that realm from the moment I arrived to let me stay, but he said that I could not—yet. As he was telling me I would have to return to my body, to earth, I was waving my arms saying, "No, no, no!" At which time I felt my spirit being sucked by what felt like a very powerful, giant, vacuum cleaner hose, but I was going through a gold tunnel that had beautiful white lights throughout (the lights were angels; I was going at such a fast rate that I could only see their light). Then BOOM! I was back in the body and in more pain than I can even begin to describe.

My parents greeted me at the hospital as the back doors of the ambulance swung open. They were crying and smiling at the same time. I said, "It's not funny, it hurts." Their response was, "We're smiling because you're alive. We thought you were dead."

For the short time I spent in the other realm, I felt more alive than I have ever felt on earth. Since the near-death experience, when I look around me, all I see are the walking dead, people who have no clue as to what is important here. Some get it, but many don't. They base their self-worth on the number of diplomas hanging on the wall, the car in the garage, the house, or their career status; sadly, they judge others based on those things as well.

For years after the accident, I had trouble adjusting, but it had more to do with the near-death experience than the injuries sustained from the wreck. The cuts and breaks all healed, but not one day has gone by that I don't relive my moments in that heavenly place—what I saw, how I felt, and what I was told. I died, went to heaven, and was pretty much tossed back into hell (earth). When I was having a particularly difficult time adjusting to life after my NDE, I would journal.

6

CHANGES IN RELATIONSHIPS

Question #6 of our survey is for the surveyee to answer "yes" or "no" to the question of "Were there any changes in your relationships / spouse / partner / friends since your NDE?"

NDErs may have changes in relationships according to the IANDS.org website: (1) they come to love and accept others without the usual attachments and conditions society expects; (2) they perceive themselves as equally and fully loving of each and all, openly generous, excited about the potential and wonder of each person they see; (3) their desire is to be a conduit of universal love; (4) confused family members tend to regard this sudden switch in behavior as oddly threatening, as if their loved one had become aloof, unresponsive, even uncaring and unloving; (5) some mistake this "unconditional" way of expressing joy and affection (heart-centered rather than person-centered) as flirtatious disloyalty; (6) divorce can result from this mistake.

Question #6 Statistics

Of the 41 Non-Gay NDErs: 35 Answered "Yes"; 6 Answered "No"
Of the 25 Gay NDErs: 19 Answered "Yes"; 6 Answered "No"

Chi-Square = 0.915772; p = 0.3386 > 0.05

Conclusion: Gay NDErs are not statistically more likely to have any changes in their relationships / spouse / partner / friends since their NDE than non-gay NDErs.

Sample NDEs

The following NDE testimony comes from a Gay NDEr who describes the changes in her relationships: I guess what I am still learning, with a great deal of difficulty, is not to take on the pain of others, no matter who they are. I can feel compassion and try to help, but most strive not to be led by my emotions and feelings, which get me into major trouble. Since no one in my family ever communicated with each other, I witnessed my sister Lucille's suffering and took on her pain, which re-directed my entire life and threw me into major depression and terror. She was the oldest and the most beautiful and brilliant of us all -- there were five girls in all. The youngest, Diane, was from another man, not from my father. My parents were divorced when I was about four-years old and we all went into an orphanage and then my mother got us back and took us back home!

To make a very long story short, my sister Lucille's journey was a very brutal one. In 1979, she froze to death in a condemned building in Coney Island where she laid on the floor for three months until someone found her (or what was left of her). I found out about it on the six o'clock news. You can imagine my horror! There are really no words to express how I felt. There are questions that will never be answered as to what really happened to her. Did she remember me, since we hadn't spoken for many years after losing touch with one another? My sister Sandy, who was in contact with her towards the end of her life, never picked up the phone and expressed concern that Lucille needed help. She also was a barrier between Lucille and her children. Lucille's daughter, Mercy (she had three girls and a boy living in Alabama) was trying to reach her and take her back home where she could have been taken care of (and would still be alive today). My sister Sandy wouldn't give me their addresses.

It took me so many years to find out where they were and to obtain their phone numbers. Sandy waited a year and half before she contacted Lucille's children and told them that Lucille died of natural causes. Since then she refuses to speak about this horrific situation. She has screamed and hollered at me for going to Alabama to meet with the children. She doesn't want anyone talking to each other because somewhere deep down inside there is guilt that she will not admit to.

We are all guilty of neglect. As you can we, my family is very dysfunctional. There are tremendous amounts of pain and scars from the past that have to heal. I am still trying to heal from the trauma. I took on my sister Lucille's pain, which shaped and almost destroyed my life. This is one of the reasons I wound up clinically dead in 1974 or thereabouts. The hospital told me my records are gone now. I don't have actual dates or anything recorded about my NDE experience of clinical death. The NDE occurred at at Bellevue Hospital, of all places -- like that terrible movie Snakepit!

The other thing I am now learning on a daily basis is to love myself and, hold myself with tenderness and know that I am truly a child of God. I am loved and deserve to have a life of quality, to laugh, to sing and to dance. My life is as important as anyone else's. I am also learning with a great deal of difficulty not to give my power away to anyone else and, after so many years, listen to my own intuition.

During the 1960's, I had an experience where the Virgin May came to me -- twice -- once at work where the whole office disappeared and once walking near 2nd Avenue and 14th Street. I lived on 2nd Avenue and 18th Street at that time. She never spoke to me, but she was shimmering in incredible colors and had a very soft and loving expression on her face. Everything -- all my surroundings -- disappeared when this happened. The Blessed Mother was surrounded by awesome colored light and peace and love was everywhere. It just about took my breath away!

My next experience was with Marilyn Monroe a year after my near-death experience -- around 1975. I was on the 1st Avenue bus going home with 400 downs (pills of every color, shape, and size) in a shopping bag to overdose again. I spoke to no one about what I was going to do. By accident I jumped up to get off the bus at my old stop on 18th street where I lived in the 1960s. In my head, I never moved out of that period of time and that apartment I loved in the 1960s.

As I was getting off the bus, I saw a black and yellow bus stop sign outside the door. I realized I was getting off at the wrong stop as I didn't live there anymore. I said to myself, "J.C. what are you doing? You don't live here anymore."

I got back on the bus all shook up as I had never done this before. I sat down in another seat and next to me was a piece of paper. I picked it up and turned it over. It was the cover of a book someone had been reading which said Norma Jean Baker. There was a picture of Marilyn Monroe on the cover. I put the paperback down and as I looked up, Marilyn Monroe was boarding the bus. She had on a long terry cloth bathrobe, deep purple, and messed-up blonde curls. She died in 1962, the year when I graduated from high school. This was 1975.

She walked up to me, we looked at each other, and she sat down next to me on my left. I knew no one else could see her but me. When I got up to get off the bus at 25th street, she followed me. We walked down the street together and up the five flights. We did not speak in public. She sat in one chair and I sat in another. She looked sad and said to me, "If you do this, you will regret it for eternity."

She said God sent her to me and she also said she wanted to come back, but she couldn't. She also said that she did not kill herself. Again, she repeated, "If you do this, you will regret it for eternity."

Just like she came to me, she got up and left right through the door. I started shaking all over and got down on my knees by the tub in the kitchen and sobbed. God spoke to me and said, "When I call for you, that's when you come to me." I got up and flushed the 400 pills down the toilet.

I am here now to speak about it. It is like getting hit with a bolt of lightning when something like this happens. I kept everything in all these years, because the few people I told said, "You're nuts!" So I stopped speaking for many years -- until 1990 when God came to me when I was ill and told me, "Speak out." I have been speaking out since then and here I am today.

Before my NDE, I was very depressed and ill from 13 shock treatments which backfired. Everything I wanted to forget I remembered bigger than life and everyday things like my address and phone numbers were all forgotten. I didn't even recognize New York City when I was released from the hospital, two blocks from my house. I lived with my boyfriend for 20 years (before and after the NDE) and it was not a good relationship. There was a lot of anguish. I was disabled with rheumatoid arthritis and, in 1990, I had a physical crisis. I was crippled in bed for six months. Then I started a detox and changed my diet with the help of my boyfriend's mother.

After detoxing and changing my diet and being so grateful to walk again and so overwhelmed that God gave me another chance, I went back to my roots. I became born again into the family of Jesus and God, like I was when I was five years old in Williamsburg, Brooklyn. As soon as I could walk, I went to Times Square Church and got baptized. I am a Messianic Jew and a believer in Jesus Christ, Amen.

While I was on my path and my boyfriend was on his, we got farther and farther apart. He became violent and attacked me physically. I wound up in a women's shelter in Brooklyn, completely traumatized. Finally after a lot of prayer, I found my lease and went to the 13th precinct in my neighborhood. I showed them my lease and told them if I didn't get my apartment back, someone would die. Four policemen escorted me to the apartment and handcuffed my boyfriend; they took him to jail. Later, I dropped the charges. Since then, we have been friends. He is bed-bound and lives around the corner from me. I shop and clean and run errands for him.

Since then, I met Robert and am very happy with him. He lives in Westchester and we go back and forth between his house and mine. In Westchester -- New Rochelle -- I listen to the birds and whistle and talk to them all the time. After feeding them sunflower seeds, sunflowers came up in the garden. Now I take care of the lawn out there, gardening for the first time in my life. This is truly a dream come true to be in the country.

Robert says, "This is not the country. It's too civilized." I love the trees and birds. What a kiss from God to grow my own sunflowers for the first time!

The following NDE testimony comes from a Non-Gay NDEr: My NDE was on 31-1-2013, the night before an ICD, internal defibrillator and pacemaker was placed in the bathroom of the university hospital in Antwerpen, Belgium. My heart pumped very weak, ejectionfraction of 15%, I went during the night to the bathroom and fell unconsciousness on the floor. For a time I didn't know I was on the floor horizontally. This time I didn't experience any sensations, seeing things, no it was physical only. Otherwise it was 4 months later when I experienced an out of body experience when I sat on a bench in my house in Middelburg, NL. I left my body and saw myself from the outside of my body. During the post operation period I suffered from extreme stress, lost my job and became violent towards my girlfriend. I never acted that way and felt very unhappy. I had to end for a period the relationship to take a grasp of myself. I spoke these times frequently with the professor J.L.F. (Hans) Gerding, who helped me process this [difficult experience.]

7

DISTRESSING AFTEREFFECTS

Question #7 of our survey is for the surveyee to answer "yes" or "no" to the question of "Were there any distressing aftereffects from your NDE?"

Studies have revealed three types of distressing NDEs (dNDEs): (1) "Inverse" dNDEs, where aspects in the dNDE which are found in positive NDEs reported as pleasurable are perceived in the dNDE as threatening; (2) "The Void" dNDEs, existential experiences of vast emptiness, darkness, often a devastating scenario of aloneness, isolation, sometimes negation of being, ego-death; (3) "Hellish" dNDEs, where the NDEr perceives overtly horrifying or hellish imagery often as an observer but sometimes experiences torment.

Responses and aftereffects of dNDEs include: (1) an enduring awareness that the physical world is not the full extent of reality; (2) personal life and social relationships are abruptly and permanently overturned; (3) adjusting to a dNDE is similar to culture shock and reactions to a dNDE are often similar to Posttraumatic Stress Disorder (PTSD); (4) aftereffects are similar to shamanic pattern of suffering / death / resurrection as an invitation to self-examination, disarrangement of core beliefs, and rebuilding; (5) not for a long time, if ever, do dNDEs cause the NDEr to lose their fear of death;

(6) the late Dr. Barbara Rommer's dNDE study concluded that, in the long run, as with pleasurable NDEs, virtually all dNDEs ultimately become extremely beneficial to the NDEr. They almost always eventually come to see their dNDE as a blessing in disguise; (7) Nancy Evans Bush (2002), a dNDEr herself, who did a study of dNDEs with Dr. Bruce Greyson, has a somewhat different view. Bush observed that the aftereffects of a dNDE is not so easy to define. She noted not one, but three categories of common response to dNDEs: (a) "The Turnaround" dNDE (e.g. "I needed that"): This response occurs when a dNDE is interpreted by the NDEr as a warning which may lead the NDEr into changing behaviors such as movement toward a dogmatic religious community where strict rules promise protection. This is the response identified by the late Dr. Barbara Rommer where the NDEr eventually comes to see their dNDE as blessings in disguise; (b) "Reductionistic" dNDE (e.g. "It was only a hallucination"): This response occurs when a dNDE allows the NDEr to repudiate the meaning of their NDE which does not fit into a safe category. Bush speculated that people in this category might find psychological peace, but only temporarily. (p. 106); (c) "The Long Haul" dNDE (e.g. "What did I do?"): This response occurs when a dNDE causes the NDEr to be "haunted" or struggle for many years with the existential implications of their dNDE. A religious element of their NDE is often expected, but is absent. This category of dNDEr is most likely to seek counseling or therapy.

Although Bush found more categories of response than Rommer did, her conclusion, like Rommer's, is optimistic: "A psychospiritual descent into hell has been the experience of saints and sages throughout history, and it is an inevitable episode in the pervasive, mythic theme of the hero's journey. Those who insist on finding the gift, the blessing of their experiences have the potential ultimately to realize a greater maturity and wholeness" (p.129).

Question #7 Statistics

Of the 41 Non-Gay NDErs: 22 Answered "Yes"; 19 Answered "No"
Of the 25 Gay NDErs: 17 Answered "Yes"; 8 Answered "No"

Chi-Square = 1.32138; p = 0.2503 > 0.05

Conclusion: Gay NDErs are not statistically more likely to have any distressing aftereffects from their NDE than Non-Gay NDErs.

Sample NDEs

One Gay NDEr wrote of being in labor and died while receiving "Pitocin drugs that maxed out and had my contractions on top of each other with no break for 12 hours. I was screaming in pain. I died; my daughter almost did. I had an emergency c-section ... when I died, I was out of my body, face first free falling in a black tunnel ... I heard what I thought was a million dragons. But I realized so fast I only had time for one word before I got to the entrance of that grey entrance. I said, 'Goddddd!!!! (God).' I immediately found myself back in myt body." Later in her next entry to this NDE presentation, she wrote of this experience as the "Hell" NDE.

One Gay NDEr responded about the nature of hell: "There is a place called "the Death Shadowed Valley," where some Souls may choose to go to if they feel too afraid, guilty or shameful to approach Heaven or God. This is an in-between place or dimension that separates Souls from this world and the next. ...And as I have discussed before ... being caught in this type of situation is a very difficult process to endure and can cause problems for both the living and the dead. However each of us has the ability to call out to God or to Christ ... and immediately ... we will be taken home to Heaven. Or we (the living) can pray and call out to God to send his Angels to come and take others home. It is important for us to understand that we each send ourselves to the places our Soul believes it most belongs. We do that now here on planet Earth. Those stuck in addiction, lust, bitterness and hate -- these are the ones truly in hell. But the moment we choose Love, we can get ourselves out. God never sends us anywhere we do not wish to stay. We have totally misunderstood the concept of hell on this planet." In response to the question about a place of burning fire, this NDEr replied, "I do know of a place in the deep regions of the Realm where I saw great caverns of electrical blue fire. However, I understood that this place was for the purpose of Loving purification. God would never send his precious creatures to a place to be burned or harmed. It is completely contrary to our Creator's nature.

Life is full of hellish experiences and God would prefer we keep ourselves from as many of these things as possible, so that we do not overly darken our Souls ... which in time will only keep us from remembering who we really are."

The following NDE testimony comes from a Non-Gay NDEr: A short description: I died during a tilt table test for 32 seconds. I remember a general dream like state and walking next to another woman. She took me to a place with no walls, no sky, and no earth. There were no indicators of location. Just white light everywhere. Many people had gathered and were very excited to see me. Before I could talk to them, the woman who brought me to this place told me to turn around. When I turned I saw a life review. I was distressed and worried I had been unkind so often. I asked my guide if I was going to hell. My guide told me that no one judges me, but me. Then, my mother stepped out of the crowd and took my hands in hers. She looked at the woman who brought me to this place and told her, "She can't stay. She has to take care of the children." I protested because I was so at peace and filled with love. For the first time in as long as I could remember, I had no physical pain. My mother said, "They need you," while pointing behind me. When I turned I saw my children through a parting in the light. I knew I was seeing them as they were right then. I had so many questions about where I was and what the future held and the answers came to me as I formed the questions in my mind. I knew everything was going to be ok. I knew I had to return and that my time here is important but temporary. Then I woke up in the testing room.

The following NDE testimony comes from a Gay NDEr who describes distressing aspects resulting from his NDE: Ego is that thing that helps us learn what LOVE is by showing us what it is not. All things on Earth must come to a place of balance. All things must have a parallel. This is how we are each caused to grow Spiritually. Just as a face (due to gravity) may wrinkle with time, so does a Soul become weighed down with ego. Ego is always LOVE'S opposite. Love raises vibration and ego lowers it. Ego is a mental essence that each of us is made to endure for as long as we walk the planet. Ego is that thing that tells us in our mind, "No you can't do that ... because you're not talented, thin, good-looking, wealthy, intelligent, young, strong, interesting or intuitive ENOUGH!" This is the voice of the Liar. The Liar is the voice of ego. Let me put it this way: wherever there is separation, condemnation, self-doubt, lack-mentality, bitterness, hostility or segregation ... you can best be sure ego is not far behind.

Ego wants to keep you earthbound and Heavenless for as long as it can. It is an essence that has been sent here to learn just as you have. However, it has a duty to challenge each of us and cause us to learn as it learns for itself. There is nothing to fear about the ego. It is just a fragile, spoiled child that screams and rants until it gets what it wants. And like any child, if you ignore it during its temper flare long enough, sooner or later it will get the message that those kinds of methods are not productive and will not yield positive results.

If you understand the ego, you will understand the concept of the devil. Satanic frequency is the LOW-RANGE frequency that surrounds us in our collective thinking. It is the opposite of the HIGH, INCOMPREHENSIBLE LOVING frequency of God. Please hear me out on something...be careful of the music you listen to, the movies or TV you watch, the gossip or negative speaking you participate in. All these things LOWER the Soul's vibration. Lower vibration brings depression, disillusionment, disease and despair. The lower our Soul's vibration falls, the more these dark things come upon us. Once you fall into LOWER vibration, immediately seek to amend it with LOVING, HIGHER VIBRATIONAL THOUGHT. It is like anything else, the more you put into something, that is what the end result will be.

8

CHANGES IN DREAMS

Question #8 of our survey is for the surveyee to answer "yes" or "no" to the question of "Were there any changes in your dreams or dream content since your NDE?"

According to Lupita Kirklin, Ph.D.: "The aftereffects of the NDE include spiritual changes and transformative mystical, alchemical states; for this particular event unchains a number of aftereffects, which in some cases are guided, not only by the NDE itself, but also by dreams containing alchemical imagery throughout the process of spiritual and personal transformation, as the NDErs adjust and integrate the NDE into their lives. Alchemical dreams contain images of an archetypal nature, representative of symbols of the process of individuation and process or production of a new centre of personality."

Here is a link to some Google images of alchemy dream symbols: http://www.google.com/search?biw=1434&bih=815&tbm=isch&sa=1&q=alchemy+dream+symbols

Question #8 Statistics

Of the 41 Non-Gay NDErs: 28 Answered "Yes"; 13 Answered "No"
Of the 25 Gay NDErs: 18 Answered "Yes"; 7 Answered "No"
Chi-Square = 0.101065; p = 0.7506 > 0.05
Conclusion: Gay NDErs are not statistically more likely to have any changes in their dreams or dream content since their NDE than Non-Gay NDErs.

Sample NDEs

The following NDE testimony comes from a Gay NDEr: It was more of a Spiritual Experience than an NDE. I used to be quick to anger, always needing to be right, and materialistic. I thought meditation would give psychic powers but I discovered something much deeper. I would see Light, have bodily tingles, a sense of detachment but also in the moment, full of Peace with an impulse to laugh. My dreams became more Spiritual with scenes of my future, meeting someone in my dream first before waking-life, meeting different types of beings and Light-Beings even receiving helpful information and advice, and I've also experienced more synchronicities. Those dreams and synchronicities were more confirmations that there is more to life than just what is physically seen and how everything is connected. I have become more empathetic but also more sensitive and sense I prefer Love-based, empathetic, connections with others, my Love may be seen as "too sensitive" or it is difficult to keep a good connection to those who are less sensitive and are more focused on a chase for more physical things.

The following NDE testimony comes from a Gay NDEr: Suicide survivor. Guardian Angel pulled me out of the tub and said it was not my time to go. Passed out for three days. Dreams of dead loved ones messages. Grandmother outside gates of heaven. Psychokinesis and Telepathy increase. Greater caring. Lost father this way. Also a paranormal and Ufologist.

The following NDE testimony comes from a Non-Gay NDEr: Horses have been my life. They have also been my death. Back in 1979, when I was 19 years old, I went out for a horseback ride in the country. Cantering down the field, my horse stumbled, and I was off the saddle in an instant and airborne. I didn't feel the impact, because I never hit the ground! I was abruptly hurled into a black velvet tunnel, at a high rate of speed. Me, the real me, detached from my body, as I was flung out of the saddle into a pitch-black dimension. One minute I was riding a horse, the next it felt like I had left the planet! My departure and death was so unexpected I couldn't comprehend my life was over when I had just begun to live. The depth of the tunnel seemed bottomless; the place I went to was limitless. I then had a powerful review of my life, too complex to write about. What I did not have was a religious epiphany, in my near-death experience: absent was heaven or hell, or any biblical references at all. Death, for me, seemed factual with an order of logical progression and profound spirituality. Also, what kept resonating throughout this experience was the concept of love, and how vital it is to be good to others. Not false kindness, but having sincere compassion for people and animals, that is what holds the most value in life. I learned all human beings are shrouded in ignorance, by design, in order to learn hard lessons through each life we live. When you die, the superficial facade falls away, and we awaken from the dream into the truth. Did this make me a better person, probably not, just more informed. I am not a vegan, new-age, kind of gal, who gives readings, or who chants and believes the universe is sending her a message. I Lura Ketchledge am an author who candidly talks about her near-death-experience.

The following NDE testimony comes from a Gay NDEr: Life in this world of suffering is but a dream within a dream. Each of us is born with a lesson to learn and a purpose for being who and what we are. My lesson has been to endure a dangerous and frightening journey across the deep and dark wild side of life until I finally found my way out into the 'Light'... After watching several 'YouTube' videos and reading doctors' opinions on the underlying causes of Near-Death Experiences (NDEs), I felt obligated to share my experience and that's why I have written this book. The incident happened almost 50 years ago when I was struck by lightning while talking on the telephone in my living room. According to the doctors who took care of me at the hospital, it was a miracle that I hadn't been physically damaged in any way. When I tried telling them about a beautiful 'Light' that I'd seen and the magnificent journey that I'd taken through the stars to reach it, none of them could give me an answer as to where I'd been. It was my home doctor who suggested that I'd possibly been momentarily dead, or at least, very close to it. Over the years since, I've described the unforgettable 'Light' to many people around the world. While some have understood, especially those with NDE experiences of their own, most have put it down to being an illusion or a hallucination.

It was during my encounter with the 'Light' that a window was opened to reveal a whole new awareness of everything within and around me. Most of what I'd been taught to believe about God and life was changed dramatically, and I became obsessed with an underlying driving desire to find something, but with no idea of what it was that I needed to look for. At the same time, my psychic senses exploded and my life became a living nightmare to the point where I contemplated suicide. Following a very powerful dreamlike premonition, successions of mysterious circumstances lead me to finding a 'Key', which had a powerful effect on my life and helped me to unlock the wisdom and strength from within that I needed to change my destiny and my poison into medicine. Later on, in the 1970s, new technologies enabled doctors to revive patients who may have otherwise died, and NDEs became commonplace throughout the world. In the 1980s, many doctors officially claimed that NDEs were fantasies programmed into the brain by Nature to take place during death and to help people deal with the dying process. For me, this news came as a huge disappointment, as my encounter with the beautiful 'Light' had not only awakened to who I truly am and my mission in life but also erased the fears and doubts that I'd always had about what comes after death.

Then, in 2003, I came across a picture taken by Hubble of the Cone Nebula that instantly took my breath away. It looked just like the beautiful multi-coloured 'Light', and I knew for certain that what some doctors had been saying regarding NDEs was wrong, especially in my case. The one thing that continued to confuse me until recent years was how I could have possibly travelled all that distance in such a short space of time, as even at the speed of light, it wouldn't have been possible. It turned out that the answer had been sitting in front of me the whole time, and it came to me the same way that so many other answers about life have manifested from within since discovering the 'Key', including the most logical and realistic explanation of 'God' and the universe ever. My life story from day one!

The following NDE testimony comes from a Non-Gay NDEr: More like an NDE like experience resulting from a fall from a horse. Didn't die but experienced NDE like things like sense of calm, quiet, peace and comfort. After that had many vivid dreams where I was standing before 'masters' in robes who, during at least two vivid dreams downloaded information about general knowledge and astrology specifically and birth times on awakening I was so happy because I now knew everything about everything and everything about astrology. But then can't remember anything. I somehow suspect that I have the knowledge somewhere and will be able to access it at some point. There are many other experiences that I've had throughout my life that have had me to question what happens after death etc. For example, as a4 year old I experienced what some would call an epiphany. Standing in front of a beautiful snowball bush in our front yard, I suddenly experienced a "knowing" that the "me that is me" will never die. It was a communication. Not a voice but a strong knowing. It affected me strongly at that young age and I think of it almost daily. My experiences are as if they happened yesterday and are still with me. There are more but I can't list them here.

9

ELECTROMAGNETIC PROBLEMS

Question #9 of our survey is for the surveyee to answer "yes" or "no" to the question of "Did you have any problems being around electromagnetic fields since your NDE?"

According to the IANDS.org website, "Electrical sensitivity refers to a condition whereby the forcefield or energy around an individual affects nearby electrical equipment and technological devices. Usually sporadic in effect and impact, some experiencers have noticed: (1) watches may stop; (2) microphones may "squeal"; (3) tape recorders may quit; (4) television channels may change with no one at the controls; (5) light bulbs may pop; (6) telephone lines may "drop off"; (7) computers may suddenly lose memory; (8) NDErs who are more at ease with their new traits report fewer of these incidents than those still in the process of making adjustments.

Question #9 Statistics

Of the 41 Non-Gay NDErs: 17 Answered "Yes"; 24 Answered "No"
Of the 25 Gay NDErs: 16 Answered "Yes"; 9 Answered "No"

Chi-Square = 3.15512; p = 0.07569 > 0.05

Conclusion: Gay NDErs are not statistically more likely to have any problems being around electromagnetic fields since their NDE than Non-Gay NDErs.

Sample NDEs

An example from one Gay NDEr explained how his NDE represented some of these issues: "When I got home, I couldn't stand any noise, TV, etc. I tried to talk but couldn't for two months. I had to be taught to walk, write, and do basic cognitive and basic skills. Several months later, I realized when I went to the supermarket, the cash registers stopped working. My watch stopped working. One night when I had recovered, I was playing in our street with the neighborhood lads. They noticed as I ran under each street light, it would go out. 'Do it again, Steve!' they begged me. Back in school, I didn't have to study as I had before. I took a test and I knew all my answers were correct, and got another A on my papers."

Another example by a Gay NDEr wrote about the post-NDE period in the following quote: "When I came back into my body, I realized how incredible our bodies are. It was like moving in molasses. I had not had that happen in the prior experience. After (this second) experience, I also had things happen that had not happened before. I could not wear a battery wrist watch. My arm ached and the battery would be dead within the day. I could not touch anything electrical. It would not work. My husband had to work the TV and VCR."

The following NDE testimony comes from a Non-Gay NDEr: I honestly do not remember many specific details. I feel my situation is unique in that I have had a few "close calls". I was born very prematurely, when I was a freshman in high school I was in a severe snowmobile accident. When I was in college, I was in a car accident. I don't remember anything other than a feeling of "flying" and waking up in my dorm room in the morning. I became very ill during my second pregnancy and my son was born with certain "awarenesses" about spiritual matters, including telling me "he has been to heaven twice" and "being in my tummy was like a sugary spaceship". He was also aware of the name of a woman who died in my parents' house several years before they bought it, and knew his grandpa Ray who passed before he was born. Since my accident, I have had a strong effect on all electronics, particularly when stressed or excited. Any extreme emotions can cause lightbulbs to blow or phones to shut off, TV to turn channels, etc. My husband is constantly fixing things. I tell people about it and they think I'm crazy or seeking attention.

The following NDE testimony comes from a Gay NDEr: I knew I liked girls in 6th grade (I am a girl). When girls would ask me which boy I liked, I would "choose" one that wasn't claimed already as "being liked." When in reality, I liked Jan. Being raised Mormon, I fought off the feelings of same-sex attraction and married a man right after high school. We had two children (I actually had 7 pregnancies but lost 5 to miscarriage). I never allowed him to do oral sex on me, because "that's how lesbians do it." I thought if I avoided anything lesbian, I wouldn't be one.

I was VERY suicidal from the time I was 16 to 44 years old (when I finally came-out). My brother killed himself at 21, my dad and I believe he was in the closet (2003). I went through three long term marriages with men, each lasting about 10 years or more. Each was a "man of God."

The first was a pedophile and sexually abused our daughter (I left him). Except for that "one" thing, he was a wonderful man and my best friend. I have no idea why he became that way.

The second was a pervert and rapist. He beat and strangled me. Our bishop (pastor) said I must not be keeping the house clean enough, giving him enough sex, having dinner on time, etc. He had Asperger's, was mild and calm most of the time. He was sexually abused by his dad. His dad went on to sexually abuse his other son's kids (his own grandkids) and went to prison (he died there).

The third one nearly beat me to death, put me in the hospital. I had to relearn to spell and write. Everyone thought he walked on water, but his PTSD from being severely beat as a child, and war PTSD made him a different man when he was under stress from his job. He took it out on me. He left me for my best friend because he wanted more children. She had five kids at home, we had no kids at home. He soon found out that he had it much better in our relationship and asked me to take him back. Nope.

While I was recovering from the head injury, I went to Unity church on a Wednesday night and saw a face that I had seen in my dreams since I was 7 years old. I had even found "look-alikes" in magazines and put them on my wall when I was a child. Parker Stevenson from the Hardy Boys TV serious was a dead match. On that Wednesday night, the world stopped and a tunnel formed around this person's face, it was the face I had seen for nearly four decades in my dreams. When I came to the present moment, I realized it was a woman! We've been married for 8 years now. I never knew a relationship could have this much kindness, love, and respect.

Where did the NDE come in? I have had 2 NDEs:

1984: The hospital wanted my labor to speed up so they gave me a Pitocin drip that was maxed out and had my contractions on top of each other with no break for 12 hours. I was screaming in pain. I died, my daughter almost died. I had an emergency c-section. My uterus was tilted back and pelvis too small to have an 8 lb 2 oz baby. When I died, I was out of my body, face first free fall in a black tunnel with a gray circle hole at the end. Falling at a 45-degree angle, down. I heard what I thought was millions of dragons. But I realized it was people screaming/whaling. It was so fast I only had time for one word before I got to the entrance of that gray entrance. I said, "GODDDDDD!!!!!!" (God). I immediately found myself back in my body.

After I healed from the c-section surgery, I looked for books about what I experienced. None existed that I could find. I got books of every religion in the world, hundreds of psychology books. I began to realize that I created my own Hell (much like the move "What Dreams May Come" with Robin Williams). I had been miserable since I was 16, a lot of self-hate. Back then Mormonism taught that you earn your way to heaven. I was always failing. Then fighting same-sex attraction was added on top of normal daily things like anger, frustration (which I was taught were sins). I think/feel I went to a place with like-minded people, other people who hated themselves and hated others (more on this in my next NDE).

1986: After the "Hell" NDE I wrote letters to every person I thought I had ever offended and said I was sorry. I tried to live in a happier, more accepting manner of myself. My husband was stationed in West Germany at the time of the second NDE. I was pregnant with my son. I was told by the doctors I was to have a second c-section, or I would die. It was a "high risk" pregnancy.

When I died: I did leave my body. It looked like I was in a black tunnel, but when I looked left and right, I could see stars. The reason it looked like a tunnel, was because at the end, almost straight up, was a round light, with rays coming out from another world or dimension. I did not go toward the light. I heard a male voice, I was not frightened or ask who he was, because he was familiar to me (I do not know who it was). The light coming out of the circle at the end of the tunnel was brilliant white light, like none that I have ever seen on earth. The most unusual thing to me was the Love, it felt like matter, like it was alive. Love permeated my whole "self." A love that was so unconditional and powerful that there are no words. The Being of Light asked me if I was "ready to die." To us that sounds creepy, to him, it was a matter of fact, a next phase (like saying, "are you ready to go home?"). I said, "What do I need to do?"

I was told three things: Love myself more, love others more, and to study the life of Jesus. Afterward, I studied the life of Jesus in the New Testament. I found a common theme of his life: unconditional love for ALL. (Not all the modern-day use of the Bible to promote slavery, hate of women, gays, etc.).

When I came back into my body, I realized how incredibly our bodies are. It was like moving in molasses. I had not had that happen in the prior experience. After this second experience, I also had thing happen that had not happened before. I could not wear a battery wrist-watch, my arm ached and the battery would be dead within the day. I could not touch anything electrical; it would not work. My husband had to work the TV and VCR. I began to know things before they happened. And I replied to people, thinking they were talking out loud. My mom began to say to me, "Do not respond to me, unless you see my mouth move, I am tired of you responding to my private thoughts!" Any board game I played, I knew the answers. Like the game Clue, my kids later refused to play with me, because I always knew "who done it." I used the gift to "sight" to help find lost pets, keys, stolen pets, etc. I never used it for personal gain.

Questions for thought: (1) I was gay my whole life, had a "hell" experience before I ever had any major sin in my life (sexual, including homosexual). My biggest downfall was self-hate. (As a good Mormon girl, I had never stolen, lied, cussed, did drugs, drank, etc.) (2) I was gay my whole life, had a "heaven" experience. No "repentance for sins," no "being saved" happened in between the two experiences. The only change between the two experiences was being loving to myself and others. (3) Does God accept gays? A person may say, "Well, you were gay, which God is ok with; you never had gay sex, so God was happy with that too." Well, why the Hell NDE? (4) Why did God place an image of that "face" in my life for nearly four decades, to only turn out to be a woman. No, it was not "friend" love feelings that was ever attached to it, it was romantic feelings.

I hear Christians say, "Well, God made gays, so it is Ok to be gay, but it is not ok to have sexual relations." That is part of the definition of being gay, emotional AND physical attraction. I do not think God made an error, or he would not have put sexual urges in gay people. If he only approved of a gay person's existence, but not their need to be in a relationship and be "one" with that person sexually, he would have not put those needs in them.

I no longer believe in "sin." I do believe in good and evil. In love and hate (including self-love and self-hate). I love the words of Jesus, but am very cautious with the words of others, especially Paul. I am a retired Hospice nurse and am getting my master's in Divinity so I can be a hospital Chaplain and assist people as they transition to the Other Side.

I am now a grandma of five. My kids have said to me that they were so blessed to have a mom who loved them with all her soul. They are now passing that legacy of love to their kids.

To answer your questions that were not already addressed above: Did I tell anyone?: I only told my husband about the NDEs. Later, I did tell my parents. My dad told me he had and NDE. I have never publicly told my story. Decades later my uncle told me about dying in surgery. I point blank asked him if he remembered when he was out of his body, he did. He told me about his NDE. I have mentioned parts of my story in chat forums in the last few years. This is the first time in 33 years I have publicly told my story in full.

Did it change my sexuality? I was able to untangle myself from the legalistic Mormon mindset and come-out to my family. The Mormon church did ex-communicate me.

Did it effect my relationships? I became calmer and kinder to people. No longer did I believe in legalistic religion where I had to earn my way to heaven. My husband believed me, as did my family.

Did your NDE include a tunnel? Yes. Did you pass through darkness in a tunnel? I stayed in the tunnel; I did not pass through it. I did not progress beyond the tunnel. Was there any sound in the tunnel? No. Were you pulled through a tunnel? No, I just floated in the tunnel, I was not pulled. Were there other people or animals in the tunnel? Just the male voice and Being of Light. Did you feel peaceful in the tunnel? Yes.

Did you experience a sort of healing? Not at that time. Later I did have a healing experience. A dead portion of my intestines was recorded on VHS via a scope put up my anus into my intestines. In one surgery, I had a GYN team of doctors and nurses to give me a hysterectomy, and a GI team of doctors and nurses to take out the black, dead 2 inches of intestines. The GI surgeon apologized afterward that he could not find the black, dead 2 inches that they still had evidence of on the VHS tape. They laid all 32 feet of my intestines out on the surgery table and could not find the dead 2 inches. I told him it was fine; I had asked my dad to give me a healing prayer the night before my surgery.

Did you merge with a light? No. Did you hear music in the tunnel? No. Did you meet a religious or spiritual leader? None that I can say by name or photo. The Being of Light I met is who I would consider as "God." Did you feel fear? No. Did any questions come to mind? No, it was very matter of fact, like I was in a place I had been before and knew all, so I did not have to ask questions. Of course, I do not remember eternal truths now that I am back here. The veil works that way. Did you have a life review? No. Did you see yourself at an earlier age? I did see myself at an older age (I was 20 at the time, I seemed to be about 35 in the "future" me, and I was shown my son (that I was pregnant with) as a grown man. Did you see yourself with other people or entities? No. Did other people or beings talk with you about your life? No. Did you see yourself or others living at another time? No. Did you have an angel with you in the NDE? Did an angel talk with you? Did an angel offer you advice? I did not have an angel with me.

Ever since I was a small girl my dad's (passed over mother) was with me. I did not know who she was until I described her to my dad when I was in my late 40s. He cried, he said that was his mom, she had committed suicide before I was born. She was by my side for decades; she was beside my bed every night as a child.

She came to me the night my dad died. She said, "Davie is with me." I had no idea who Davie was. I called my mom. She said that was my dad's nick name given to him by his mom when he was little. I had only heard him called David or Dave. Mom confirmed that dad had just then passed away. That same night my dad came and just stood quietly beside my bed. We had promised each other, that whoever went first, we would go see the other one.

Describe your dreams since your NDE: Psychic type dreams in color. I think all the other questions were already part of my story.

10

CHANGES IN SENSITIVITY TO LIGHT

Question #10 of our survey is for the surveyee to answer "yes" or "no" to the question of "Were there any changes in sensitivity to light since your NDE?"

Light and sound are waves having a particular frequency. According to the IANDS.org website: (1) Sensitivity to light and sound can be a serious issue and may necessitate some lifestyle changes; (2) While most NDErs learn to limit sunshine exposure, others can't get enough; (3) Almost everyone, though, has similar difficulties with loud or discordant sounds; (4) Many NDErs can no longer tolerate "hard" rock music. The vast majority prefer classical, melodic, and/or natural sounds, and become passionate about using music to heal.

Question #10 Statistics

Of the 41 Non-Gay NDErs: 22 Answered "Yes"; 19 Answered "No"
Of the 25 Gay NDErs: 15 Answered "Yes"; 10 Answered "No"
Chi-Square = 0.25354; p = 0.6146 > 0.05

Conclusion: Gay NDErs are not statistically more likely to have any changes in sensitivity to light since their NDE than Non-Gay NDErs.

Sample NDEs

One Gay NDEr wrote: "In my NDE, the first thing I noticed was I was no longer in pain. Then I was surrounded in a brillant white light almost unbearable to look at ... I was floating in white clouds, not touching any ground ... Seven angels appeared around me. I was in the middle. They were all in brilliant white robes with hoods on." He continued, "After I joined the angels again, after my enjoying the looks, I asked them 'Was it okay for me being gay?' I was assured, 'There was nothing wrong with being gay.' Being gay or not was like the difference between having blue eyes or brown eyes."

One Non-Gay NDEr wrote, "Remembering my light-experience consists of a unique 'knowing and feeling' that I have not experienced again in any other earth-event. In my concluding years here on planet Earth, I am filled with a 'peace and joy' that can only come from the 'infinite, unconditional loving light.'" Later in his response, he explained, "Then I remembered that my drowning was my passage back into the Light."

The following NDE testimony comes from a Gay NDEr: My experience occurred at about 6.40pm, 1 December 2012. I must tell you what an enormous relief it is to come across your website Liz. I have had terrible problems since the experience with nobody around me having experienced the same. They simply cannot share the same priorities I have if they have not experienced it. I feel such urgency to find people who understand.

So I wish to first acknowledge what an important thing you are doing. Near-death experiences offer the clearest reporting of what happens beyond birth and death. Free from any religious or spiritual 'selling', you can report on people's direct experiences. This is perhaps the most crucial work a person can do at this time, to collate the evidence and work out ways for people to return to the Light.

I will elaborate. Sigh. I hope you will not discard me simply because I made the near-death experience happen myself. That is, it occurred during a meditation retreat session. But I guarantee you it was exactly the same as someone who physically dies. I propose to describe it in such detail that any reasonable person will be convinced. I actually feel special that this happened to me in meditation, although the actual crossing over was a gift. You will see what I mean.

I am a rainbow male. I do not identify with the word gay. This word was given to me by a society that historically has harmed people like me. We are an overpopulated planet. It has only been by researching individuals in indigenous cultures such as the Maori people of New Zealand, that I have understood that when there was enough space for tribes to feed off the surrounding land sustainably, there was a treasured place for people like us. More on that later.

As a little boy I knew that I was connected to the light. I delighted in rainbows constantly, drawing them, painting them, wearing them and watching them dance on my bedroom walls after refracting through a crystal.

Today I would say that as a baby I was abiding in the consciousness available inside the innermost chamber of my heart. My parents were quite mind-driven, I would say, trying desperately to provide for me and my sister. I knew that I was the cause of their suffering, to some extent. So I clenched the innermost chamber of my heart shut with the thought that I was ugly and disgusting. I knew that my inherent nature was not what they were trying to cultivate in me.

So I always had this burning desire to know the Truth. What happens when we die? What is the true purpose of being human? What is the purpose of being gay? Nobody around me seemed to have the answers, certainly not from their own experience anyway. A generation of rainbow males before me died out without my even being aware of them. Nearby, in houses of nearby suburbs they quietly and secretly died of AIDS. I was shielded from my own community, my own lineage.

I come from two English bloodlines but was raised in Christchurch, New Zealand. My mother protected me from my distant father and some of the school bullying. But I knew somehow that any true answers would have to be found by me. So I started reading near-death experiences.

The following NDE testimony comes from a Non-Gay NDEr: I had a blood clot formed by AFib go into my heart whilst having surgery to remove it from my arm. I went into full Cardiac Arrest three times when I was at the hospital. As the 3 incidences occurred over several hours, I was awake and alert when the last two happened. The second time everything just went out and I woke up from what I can only describe feeling like I was hit in the head with a baseball bat. The 3rd time once again the lights seemed to go out but his time I felt like I was being pulled. I remember being in a very bright place that seemed it could be endless. There were "beings?' near me that communicated to me that I wasn't ready. I seemed to have been in this place a very long time. Then I came back and and was put out out by the doctors. The place I went to was like a way station. I think and feel it was a place you went before you are reincarnated. I never believed in this before but my thoughts have somewhat changed on the subject. I have pretty much made a full recovery but that last experience has stayed with me as though it just happened.

The following NDE testimony comes from a Non-Gay NDEr: I suffered from sleep apnea. I awoke to find myself outside my house sort of floating toward a neon white being in a robe. I felt this being hold me in a very loving way. Behind this being I saw what looked like capsules of light coming up off of the ground in the distance. They seem to be flying up into space. Then there was a fog, gray / blue and I found myself in the center of it, spinning around and what felt like a whirlpool of love. There were also something that looked like golden sparkles that I saw while this was happening. The feeling was of great love. Then I guess the experience ended, as I found myself in taking a humongous, painful intake of breath like I had never done before. After this experience I never had any more problems with sleep apnea.

The following NDE testimony comes from a Non-Gay NDEr: I was a small boy and not yet able to swim. I went into the pool alone, and I drowned. After initial panic, I calmed and noticed a light. I was trying to figure where the light was coming from, and the noticed I was in a dark void. An amorphous being of immense love and compassion told me that it was not my time, and I had things that I had to accomplish. I was sent back. That is all that I remember.

The following NDE testimony comes from a Non-Gay NDEr: During finals week of the 4th quarter of chiropractic college, I went over to a friend's house to study. A woman fell asleep driving towards me and crashed into my car. I rose above the accident and said: "Oh my God, I can't die yet, I still have to finish my finals!" Archangel Michael came into view and said, "Anlee, you have another school to go to first. Don't worry; I'll return and finish my chiropractic college." "I go by Annie now; nobody can pronounce Anlee right!" "We know of the problem, but we know you by your given name." I feel I'm just a thought, no physical body to slow us down, I'm quickly escorted into my twin flames arms, then off to a University in Nirvana. Powerfully a loving acceptance and support welcomed everyone. I absorbed healing with Source's Light in my dying physical body and how we can access healing by adjusting our internal narrative, through accepting our connection with Source. The extended event is in the final stages of a manuscript for publication soon.

The following NDE testimony comes from a Non-Gay NDEr: Car crash whilst on body guard assignment. Car lost control hit trees, bounced, cleared the road, hit more trees, then ended its journey 1.4 of a mile from where it began, upside down in a ditch, with a collapsed roof, and a tree penetrating the car, smashing in through the dashboard, destroying the head restraint. Barely managed to extract myself. but later the Police took me to the mangled wreck, and asked me if I was the driver, as the tree had continued inwards and I should have been decapitated! Walked away with scratches. To this day I personally recall being taken from the car to watch the accident unroll before my very eyes, and sensed two pillars of pure light either side of me, until the car stopped, and I was back inside of it thinking I was dead!

11

PSYCHOLOGICAL CHALLENGES

Question #11 of our survey is for the surveyee to answer "yes" or "no" to the question of "Were there any psychological challenges since your NDE?"

According to the IANDS.org website, some of the major characteristics of psychological changes, which may or may not be challenges, include: (1) the ability to easily engage in abstract thinking; (2) becoming more philosophical; (3) "inner child" or unresolved issues from childhood tend to surface; (4) an increase in intuitive / psychic abilities plus the ability to know or "re-live" the future; (5) the rejection of previous limitations in life and "normal" role-playing; (6) the continuing ability to dissociate or "separate" from the body; (7) the ability to be easily absorbed or "merge into" whatever is being focused on; (8) forming expansive concepts of love while at the same time being challenged to initiate and maintain satisfying relationships; (9) becoming more detached and objective; (10) going through various bouts with depression.

Question #11 Statistics

Of the 41 Non-Gay NDErs: 28 Answered "Yes"; 11 Answered "No"
Of the 25 Gay NDErs: 19 Answered "Yes"; 6 Answered "No"
Chi-Square = 0.450011; p = 0.5023 > 0.05
Conclusion: Gay NDErs are not statistically more likely to have any
psychological challenges since their NDE than Non-Gay NDErs.

Sample NDEs

The following NDE testimony comes from a Gay NDEr: I am a very
different person than who I was at 19 years old. I was a lost young man
who had what felt like insurmountable roadblocks to a happy life in my
way, and I had no tools to repair those issues, like most 19-year-old young
men. I am a black man in a white man's world, and at age 19, it was just
becoming very clear to me how much more difficult it was going to be to
get anywhere in life than it was for my friends who were 90% white, and
it was really starting to depress me seriously.

I have always dealt with depression from the time I was a young boy.
My father passed away when I was 12, and I had never dealt with his loss
in a healthy way. When he died, my Mother was completely unprepared
how to manage our lives alone. We had to leave our nice suburban life in
Oxnard, California, and move in with family in Long Beach, it was like
moving to another planet for a 12-year-old. I was also just beginning to
figure out I was gay, and as puberty took hold, the depression became
severe. I contemplated suicide because I was terrified if I was gay that my
Mother would truly hate me, and the rest of my family would as well. My
family has a very negative attitude about gay people, and the pressure I
was feeling to "fix myself" was overwhelming. I took pills out my Mom's
medicine cabinet once to try to "OD" when I was 14, and all they did was
cause me to take a short nap. I did know they were only allergy medication,
which is sort of funny in hindsight.

Barely a year out of high school, I was in Los Angeles to see my friend
who had moved there to attend UCLA. On a bitter cold Saturday night

he had got us a room at this gay hotel because he wanted to buy Meth, and that was the best place to find it he said. He was right, and within an hour we had scored the drugs and were hanging out in our room. I was not a drug user before this, but I couldn't see the point of not trying it, once he brought it up. As the evening progressed my friend told me he was "slamming it" on weekends. He explained that meant shooting it in your vein, like a hardcore drug addict. As repulsed as I was by the idea of doing it, I sat there and watched him do it to himself, and was fascinated by his physical response to doing it. He became flushed and it looked he was feeling euphoria, and he kissed me for the first time, and I wanted to feel like he was feeling. He said he could do it for me, and I let him. I guess I did not understand that he was so messed up, he lost track of what he was doing and put way too much of the Meth in the liquid mixture, he told me later he had intended to make two doses, but somehow combined them together.

As he shot it into my vein in my arm, as soon as he released the rubber tie around my arm, I felt it move through me, but instead of feeling euphoria, I fell down with a thud and lay on the floor, unable to speak in a cold sweat. After a few minutes I started shivering and shaking like I was freezing cold, unable to ask for help, I later was told I had gone into shock. My friend was freaking, but trying to keep it together. He wrapped me up in a blanket on the floor and called someone to ask for help. That is the last thing I remember as I drifted off.

Suddenly I was above my body, hearing my friend crying uncontrollably. I wanted to tell I him was okay but how? Then I saw above me this light, I knew I was dead but I had no intention of going into that light because I knew it would mean I would die, and I wasn't ready. Then I felt a presence and I knew who it was before I saw him, it was my Dad. Standing in front of me, I finally felt okay about dying. I wanted to wrap my arms around him and cry from happiness, so I did.

He said, "Son, you need to start to forgive yourself for things you cannot change, you must love yourself so others can love you and you must stop allowing other people to tell you who you are." I told my dad I didn't want to live anymore, I wanted to be with him and he said "You have so much to do still, you are going to fall in love and be a Dad yourself someday and I cannot let you cheat yourself out of that, you deserve to have that life." I tried to tell him I was gay, and that life could never be mine. He said "I know you are gay, son, I have always known. Everything I said that will be yours, will be, as long as you live and work for it".

Then he moved towards my friend, who still sobbing, he leaned into his ear and said: "Maybe I should try CPR on him". Then my Dad smiled at me, told me he will always be with me and loved me more than anything else in the universe, at that moment I woke up on the floor with my friend above me, doing CPR on me.

It took a long time to process this experience, but the changes it made in my life were immediate. I never touched drugs ever again! I have no idea what happened to my friend from that night, we lost touch because of that event, it was too much for us both to deal with and stay friends.

I was freed from the pressure of trying to be someone I am not. I accepted who I am and developed an attitude toward my family that was "I love me, and I refuse to allow you to effect that, so if you cannot accept me as who I have always been, then I will miss you". I said these exact words to my Mother, and after some time to think about it, she chose to stay in my life, and today we are closer than ever. I also finally started taking medication for my depression for the first time and went to a therapist about my issues, which was life-changing for me. My Mom was at my side as my "best man" when I married the love of my life in 2016. She is going to be a Grandma in a few months, and she has never been happier. Everything my Dad said would be, was true, I just didn't realize in 2008, he meant I could marry a man and it would be legal! I know Heaven and God are real, and I pray every day for guidance because of it, but mostly, when I hear that little voice in my ear, boy do I pay attention now!

The following NDE testimony comes from a Gay NDEr: How does one do spiritual warfare? My answer might surprise you. Spiritual warfare is a practice of celebration. Why? Because celebration is the very opposite to depression which is what dark energies want us to fall into so they can tighten their grip on us.

Dark energies do not want us to celebrate and rejoice in the fact that beyond any truth ... God is Love and God's Love has already won and achieved victory over any challenge that might come against us. It is up to us to open ourselves up and receive God's Love ... All we must do is simply ... believe!

The dark forces of challenging energy come to steal our Joy! The reason for this is because misery Loves company! Ever notice that? People who are in the habit of being down adore it when others come and join them in their destructive pity party. Well, these "sad parties" are for the most part attended by darkened energies. Because dark energy is joyless, it wants us to become the same! However, never forget ... the Joy of the Lord is our Strength!

When you feel as if you are being overcome by shadow ... it is time for you to announce "NO MORE!" and celebrate your life! I highly recommend that during times when you feel something evil is trying to sneak up on you from the back door, swing open the front door and let the Light of God's Love come in your life in every way you can think of or Holy Spirit shows you. Throw out all behaviors you know to be destructive and unpositive. Allow no negative conversation to come from your mouth! Only affirm the positive!

Hint: Turn off the TV... and put on the CD player! Use music to heal your life! Keep in mind that when we go back home to Heaven, music is what God uses to restore our Souls! Powerful and stirring music is everywhere! If we are wise, we will play good Love affirming music in our environments often! I use everything from Gospel to Enya. Play that wonderful music in your homes, cars and work spaces every day. Think of it as a can of Lysol that not only helps to disinfect your space from dark energy, it spreads colorful rainbow Light for you to walk into.

Sometimes i feel so ashamed because of my weaknesses! Never allow shame to come down on you because you have fallen into challenge. Every person on this planet has to endure this process and every person has been made stronger because of it. The occurrence of challenge is a part of God's perfect plan. Most think that they have to make themselves perfect before God will have anything to do with them. This is not so. It is our challenges in life that help us to find him! Once we get past our challenges, we understand the great unconditional Love he has for us and he uses our experiences to help dislodge others who are stuck in the same places we have been.

What happens to me spiritually once I am able to have victory over a challenge? Each time we are able to build our Light back up, we then add solid muscle to our Souls. I am speaking of spiritual muscle (made of dense Light) which will help us to lift up issues and challenges that might have been impossible to get through before. It is through this method that God prepares us to undertake our life's mission. This is why many people have difficult lives before they come into their glory. The challenges they faced will have strengthened them to the degree that once they arrive at their Divine destination, very little will be able to shake them.

What are some things you should watch out for? Never allow hatred to exist within you! Do all you can to remove it from your life. Hatred is the greatest toxin known to humankind. Never allow yourself to remain angry. Anger brings disease and challenging energy. Do all you can to avoid excess. Excessive food, drink, lust, intoxicants, ambitious planning, competition, and (of course) grief, bitterness, resentment and judgment. The gray energies can easily fool us into becoming unbalanced if we over indulge in any one person, place, thought or thing. Be sure to get plenty of fresh air, exercise, rest and watch what poisons (unnatural substances) you put into your body. Drink plenty of water. Your spirit wants to help you wash toxins out of your body. Water was made for this purpose. Your body is the temple for the Spirit. The ego will do all it can to have you disrespect yourself so that you might ultimately lose your sense of importance and Divine worth. Beware of the ego at all times and look for it in all situations and people. Once you spot ego, ask God to help you assume spiritual control. Never be ashamed to ask for God's help. He is right there waiting to show you the way out of your dilemma. Seek to be respectful to all living creatures. Be generous whenever you can. Remember that Mother Earth has been a gracious host, let us do all we can to keep her a wonderful place for our children to live.

How did my near-death experience affect your music career? When I came back from my NDE, I made a promise to myself that I would only record and sing songs that had a positive and healing influence on the Soul. So far, I have kept that promise and I'm honored to hear from those who tell me they play my music in their homes, cars, at work and in their healing spaces every day or at least several times a week. It pleases me greatly to hear from these folks and then find out that the music is helping them to heal from trauma, break spells of depression ... or motivate and cause positive momentum in their lives!

Music filled with strong flowing melodic lines, lush tones and positive lyrics can cause us to become filled with Light thus enhancing our ability to give and receive Love. Because God is actually part MUSIC, good positive music can greatly help us maintain a sense of connection and union with our eternal Spirit.

After my NDE, I came back fully understanding the power music has over our lives; as God gifted me with an ability to be sensitive to tones held within the music. Now I have an advanced capacity to comprehend what tones are secretly communicating to the Soul. I use this ability when I write, arrange and produce mine (and other's) music. In fact, that is why I typically write the melody first and then put the words down later. For me, music is a message waiting for a translation. An artist is a person whom God has blessed with a tremendous emotional vocabulary to communicate to others (who are still developing their impressions about the world that surrounds them.)

In my NDE, I learned that dark tones and harshly/suggestively sung music (with negative lyrics) listened to over time, makes our mind and Soul progressively distressed and dysfunctional. Usually the artists doing these kinds of songs are typically distressed and dysfunctional themselves. It is because of this that I strongly advise people who are working on fixing their lives or staying on a Light filled path, to stay as far away from such music as much as possible! Unfortunately, much of the "popular music" in today's culture is littered with destructive lyrics and non-nurturing tones. Without being aware, the general public has been trained by the greed-based media to actually become entertained by dysfunctional songs, and most people (especially youth) have no clue that much of the music (they are listening to) is actually injuring them emotionally! Some may have an inkling of this fact, but because of media hypnotism, socialized peer pressure, boredom or lack of quality music ... they listen anyway. And we wonder why we have so much violence, materialism, uncontrolled lust and other issues? From what I now understand spiritually, the TV and the radio has just about done modern day culture in! And if we don't start becoming more observant to the negative programming we are filling our minds with day after day, we are going to be caused to become numb to what is actually good for us and not be able to make effectual and lasting "positive" momentum in our lives! We have to train ourselves to pay close attention to how the music we are listening to makes us feel. Does it make us feel peaceful, joyous or dynamic? Or does it leave us feeling aggressive, resentful, bitter, lustful or arrogant? Be careful! Music is powerful stuff. It can either help heal you or hurt you. With all my Heart I advise you to listen wisely!

12

REINTEGRATION DIFFICULTIES

Question #12 of our survey is for the surveyee to answer "yes" or "no" to the question of "Was there any difficulty reintegrating after your NDE?"

According to the IANDS.org website: (1) One of the reasons life seems so different afterward is because the experiencer now has a basis of comparison unknown before; (2) Familiar codes of conduct can lose relevance or disappear altogether as new interests take priority; (3) Such a shift in reference points can lead to a childlike naivete; (4) With the fading of previous norms and standards, basic caution and discernment can also fade; (5) It is not unusual to hear of NDErs being cheated, lied to, or involved in unpleasant mishaps and accidents; (6) Once they are able to begin integrating what happened to them, discernment usually returns.

Question #12 Statistics

Of the 41 Non-Gay NDErs: 28 Answered "Yes"; 13 Answered "No"
Of the 25 Gay NDErs: 23 Answered "Yes"; 2 Answered "No"
Chi-Square = 4.97017; $p = 0.02579 > 0.05$

Conclusion: Gay NDErs are not statistically more likely to have difficulty reintegrating after their NDE than Non-Gay NDErs.

Sample NDEs

The following NDE testimony comes from a Non-Gay NDEr: On my birthday July 25 this year I became sick and went into the E.R. and they gave me a pain shot and told me I had the flu and sent me home. When I was leaving I became very dizzy hardly could walk. I got into my car to go home and I saw myself sitting in the passenger seat telling myself how to make it home safe. I get home I couldn't speak just lied on my bed watching everyone talking to me I felt paralyzed and and scared. I am standing next to myself trying to get someone to notice something was wrong! Everyone left to let me rest but I followed them asking for help and no one heard me. The next day my friend took my temperature in the afternoon because I was out the whole time and it was 104.6 she rushed to the hospital where I was very ill.

The following NDE testimony comes from a Non-Gay NDEr: I flatlined post surgery, was in a coma for a month. I remember not being able to breath then I had a series of "trips". I'm sorry but I don't think you need to know the rest to put in some book. Perhaps my story is different due to actually going VSA, but there were no angels, no resulting super powers or insights, no talks with religious icons no bright light. I did see a friend that died the same day though. The fact is I don't believe most of the formulaic stories I have read on your site. They are all the same like a repeated fairy tale. No one has ever mentioned their nails falling out or scars disappearing. The only problems I had were from the colostomy bag. Good luck finding someone who will really knows what it's like to make the change.

The following NDE testimony comes from a Non-Gay NDEr: Drowning on a beach knocked breathless by an ocean wave at age 5. No struggling to get up, experienced tranquility love and may have been OBE since I have a clear picture of a child floating face down. Live review was in a flip book format. No recall of transfer elsewhere or back. Remember thinking during life review "well this isn't going to take very long, I'm only FIVE." The next recollection is being hauled up by the crossed strap and hair by an adult and being set on my feet coughing and sputtering. I am highly empathic since childhood, with no fear of death/dying. Have had definitive OBE and telepathic thought reception experiences when older.

The following NDE testimony comes from a Non-Gay NDEr: I was two. Dying of liver failure. Died. Went to heaven. Saw Jesus and God sitting on white thrones. Jesus told me I could not stay and sent me back. My mother was hiding me when I stopped breathing and died. She prayed over me and asked God not to take me.

The following NDE testimony comes from a Non-Gay NDEr: I am lucky to say that I have had many lives this life. I drowned as an infant, i fell down a cliff some 30 metres high, i rolled down 200mtrs of road in a car, i was beaten unconscious for several days, i have had massive electric shock. Each time, i was aware of what was happening and felt that i was thrown out of my body. I have experienced OOB experiences fairly frequently. The latest was at age 43 where the complete leaving the body whilst in a consciously aware state and knowing what was to happen.

The following NDE testimony comes from a Non-Gay NDEr: My story feels very convoluted to explain, however I think you're asking regarding what I remember from the experience itself, and that is what I will limit this explanation to. I began vomiting rather violently and was brought to the local hospital ER where I went into torsades des pointes and cardiac arrest. They told me I was dead for between a minute and minute and a half. I remember moving extremely fast, faster than anything describable but there was no fear of speed, I was becoming part of "love" / "joy" / "peace". I was shown places that I'd always wished to see on Earth, like hovering for however long it took for me to take in the majesty and awe before being instantly brought to the next. All the while I was becoming more and more "love"... I don't think I was meant to come back necessarily... The pain of being brought back to the physical dimension was excruciating, both physically and spiritually, as I've searched for someone to talk to who can relate to the changes from this experience; which have been both challenging ~ and yet also truly amazing.

13

CHANGES IN INTERESTS

Question #13 of our survey is for the surveyee to answer "yes" or "no" to the question of "Were there any changes in your jobs / school / interests or hobbies?"

According to Dr. Bruce Greyson and Dr. Kenneth Ring's study into "Life Changes Inventory - Revised" changes in the NDErs may include: (1) changes in concern for material things of life; (2) changes in interest in creating a good impression; (3) changes in competitive tendencies; (4) changes in ambition to achieve a high standard of living; (5) changes in the desire to become a well-known person; (6) changes in the interest in what others think of you; (7) changes in the interest in achieving material success; (8) changes in concern for social values; (9) changes in concern with the welfare of the planet; (10) changes in concern about the threat of nuclear weapons; (11) changes in concern with ecological matters; (12) changes in interest in political affairs; (13) changes in concern with questions of social justice.

Question #13 Statistics

Of the 41 Non-Gay NDErs: 31 Answered "Yes"; 10 Answered "No"
Of the 25 Gay NDErs: 22 Answered "Yes"; 3 Answered "No"
Chi-Square = 1.50733; p = 0.2195 > 0.05
Conclusion: Gay NDErs are not statistically more likely to have any changes in their jobs / school / interests or hobbies than Non-Gay NDErs.

Sample NDEs

The following NDE testimony comes from a Non-Gay NDEr: On August 13, 1974, Palden Jenkins (www.palden.co.uk) and an Australian named Paul, a very close friend and "soul-brother," ate a bunch of wild herbs -- one of which was Hemlock Water Dropwort, Europe's most poisonous plant. When Paul began to get extremely sick, Jenkins told Mike's wife to get help at the nearest house which was a half-a-mile away. Fortunately, Jenkins had first aid training and was able help Paul somewhat. Unfortunately, they were 30 to 40 miles away from the nearest hospital in Snowdonia, North Wales. As Jenkins was looking after Paul, Jenkins started to get sick himself and lose consciousness. The next thing Jenkins knew he woke up in the hospital after being unconscious for eight days. Unfortunately, Paul died of a brain hemorrhage due to the Hemlock's enormous nerve poison. Later, Jenkins underwent hypnotic regression during which he discovered he had a near-death experience while he was sick and unconscious. The following is his NDE testimony while under hypnosis:

"In the inner world, Paul and I were walking hand in hand towards the Pearly Gates. It really was the Pearly Gates! I never knew the Pearly Gates actually existed, but they did -- at least, in my experience. The wise guardian of the gate came. He welcomed us and addressed Paul. This wise being said some things to Paul such as, 'Off you go. Go in through the gates.'

"I was about to follow and he said, 'Stop! You're not finished yet.'

"I think he told me some things that I have no way of remembering what he said. I just remember the feeling of it.

"I underwent a kind of panic and disorientation because, at that particular moment, I was quite relieved to be out of this life business and going in to the Pearly Gates. That was alright by me. So I was a bit panicked to be told it wasn't going to happen. It was as if this being kind of just fixed me in an energy field." (I've found I can do this sometimes. For example, with Tulki, my son, there are times when Tulki loses it and I can kind of fix him in an energy field and he'll immediately just straighten up.)

"Then he fixed me. He said something like, 'The whole of your self is going to dissolve,' or words to that effect, 'and you are going to become something different.' It wasn't exactly words, but that's the kind of impression.

"I was calmer, but still a little bit disoriented. I had enough of the experience of near-death from a couple of accidents earlier in life and I knew that the best thing to do at the moment was to let go. Let be. And so I did just that.

"Then there was this beautiful experience. I was standing there as if this cloud of diamond fog (mist, diamond mist) kind of separated me from within myself. My selfhood kind of evaporating upwards - disappearing upwards into the Void. It was as if my being was just being lifted up. My pain and the human woes were getting lifted up. It was one of those feelings of 'Aahhhhh! Aahhhhhh!' (sounding hugely relieved).

"Then there was a pause. He (the wise guardian) was still standing in front of me and had me fixed in an energy pod -- a non-visible energy pod. Then suddenly it was as if another person suddenly dropped into me from above. It just came 'joomph!' into me. It occupied my body. At that very moment (this gets confusing now), the old me just went 'pop!' It kind of popped out to the side -- back and to the side.

"Suddenly (now this is the interesting bit), it (the other person) was standing perhaps a yard behind the body or energy-body that was me. The remarkable thing was that I was experiencing this from both places at the same time. The first experience was the me that had popped out. The second experience was the me into which this being had plopped. I was experiencing it simultaneously. I've experienced this since then in various ways. Because I do quite a lot of inner work nowadays, I experienced this since then. There was a poignant moment where the being that plopped out (I can remember the thought going on) thought, 'Well, what happens now?'

"I didn't feel as if anything bad was going on. There was a very matter-of-fact feeling to it; but, in another way it was like, 'Whoaa!' It was amazing.

"Then the Pearly Gates gentleman said something to me to indicate or instruct me in what I needed to do next.

"Then, I was in my etheric body and I was still me; but, I was over there as well. I reached in to my heart and reached straight in to my heart. As I did that, it was as if there was a spark. I can only call it a static, stationary spark. It was totally of the nature of a spark but it was not sparking. I hope this is making sense!

"I reached in and just took hold of the spark and I pulled it out of myself. It was almost like it was the length of my body. It was a very strange experience because I was totally willing for this to happen. But it was very weird, because I was taking my life essence out. Myself! And the heart was the nexus of it. I don't know if anything intervened. I don't think anything came in at that time, but basically, I took that spark and I just inserted it and pushed it in to the other me.

[Note: Jenkins experience with the "spark" pulled from his "etheric body" is a good description of the so-called "silver cord". The rest of Jenkins' testimony is a question and answer session with his hypnotherapist.]

Hypnotherapist: "The one that popped out?" Paul Jenkins: "No. The one that had popped out was the me I've just been talking about from which I took the spark. I was putting the spark into the me that was still there - the me that had the other being who'd plopped into me, right?

"It was a little bit tricky. It involved some fitting and I had to do it quite carefully. It was as if there were thought waves coming from the Pearly Gates gentleman as well, who was helping and guiding this, but it was me doing it. I had to fit this into the other me. Now at the same time, I was experiencing this from the other me. And I was experiencing (This is confusing) both."

Hypnotherapist: "You were both?" Palden Jenkins: "Yes, I was both. I was both doing it and being done to.

"There was a point where it just went 'click!' It clicked in. Suddenly I could feel a slight bias of consciousness toward the me that had plopped out at that stage. But suddenly the consciousness clicked over to the other one much more, and so I was still conscious of the me that had popped out, but less so. It was as if the center of gravity of consciousness had shifted into the being out of whom I had popped and into which this other being had dropped. But the thing was, this other one who came in was me."

Hypnotherapist: "That makes sense. That's how I've always thought of walk-ins - as another aspect of yourself."

Palden Jenkins: "Well, the way I came to understand it a bit later on, was as if we were brother souls. Actually, I use that word quite consciously to put in the masculine. In fact, I had some imagery (this is digressing a bit) where it was as if we were brother souls with a long-term specialist contract. The contract was that we were like marathon-runners and handing over the baton whenever necessary."

[Note: Jenkins could be describing Paul as his "soulmate".] Palden Jenkins: "I had reached a dead end in my awakening. I think it was possibly do to the use of acid and psychedelics in the 60s, but not in the negative, judgmental way that a lot of people would think. There was nothing going wrong; but the problem was, I was no longer going to be able to integrate into the modern world properly. I had gone off too much. I was still sane. But in a sense, I was in the 14th century or prehistoric times or somewhere else. I was not going to be able to integrate again - this was the insight I got. So I needed to be re-booted and have some parts replaced.

"So there was this transfer of this, what I can only call, life-energy or life-spark. I was very aware that as soon as it clicked in, that being into whom it had clicked (who was me) was suddenly energized. I got an image here of Commander Data of Star Trek. There's a part of me which is a bit like Data in a way. Sometimes I go into this super-brain kind of consciousness which is a bit like Data. I've even got that little turn of the head sometimes. It was as if the being that had just received the spark suddenly just clicked. Also, my consciousness had shifted over. I was still in two but the center of gravity had shifted."

Hypnotherapist: "Was there anything else?" Palden Jenkins: "There was some sort of interaction between these two selves. It was as if we were saying, "Hello." It was a bit like some of the imagery that comes up in my life is about SAS work (Special Operations). It was a bit like we had met in the middle of the wilderness and there were some messages to get over before we parted company again. It was one of these quick five minute intense exchanges where this essential exchange had to go on with no niceties and no cups of tea. But it was through thought. Then there came a point where that came to a completion.

"Then, from the viewpoint of the me who had hopped out and then given its spark away, suddenly I felt as if the plug was pulled out. I started evaporating - dematerializing. There was this slightly tingly diamond evaporation. It was quite blissful - intensely blissful. That part of myself was dissolving - dematerializing. As soon as the spark had been given over and the essential exchanges had been made, there was no longer a purpose for that soul to be a constituted soul. So it just started evaporating. Now I was watching it from my other side or self.

"There was a feeling of an 'out-of-your-body and your-body's-been-really-cold' deathly kind of sense. Then you come back in and perhaps you've had a hot drink or perhaps someone's given you a massage or something like that and you can feel the life-energy gradually filling your body. You can feel the systems coming up again - the warmth rising. There was an experience like that.

"Now I'm a single being but I've got a new (the same body) personality with many of the same brain-thoughts and things like that. I've got a new (what I can only call) soul, but that's not an adequate word for what had popped inside me. It was anchored by this spark which had activated the system and reintegrated it into one being. I was quite also surprised at the comfort of that.

"That's where I think this business of brother souls comes in. It's as if it was all very finely pre-calculated so that it would all exactly work. It was fascinating.

"Then I was with this Pearly Gates man, and he was giving me some quite lengthy instructions which (you know how it is in dreamtime; time is a very difficult thing to estimate.) was probably ten minutes of teachings or instructions or exchanges. Then it was over.

"Suddenly, there was this process starting up where there was a rumble and a feeling that I was starting to get heavier. Then there was this faaalling ... faaalling ... aaaaaaah ... kind of feeling. A feeling of going into the soup - going down into the thickness.

"There was an element in me of reluctance - but not exactly. It was the same feeling I had experienced in the pre-birth experience as well - a poignant mixture of reluctance and willingness - kind of 'job-to-be-done' approach to things. It was kind of a, 'Right lads, come on. We've got to get on with it and the sooner we get this over with the better.' That kind of approach. I've always been like that really.

"I'm a Virgo - a very Saturnine Virgo. I've always been somewhat unwilling to be alive. But I also know that there is no alternative until the job's done and that I would regret it if I did otherwise. It's that kind of strange poignant mixture. This was the reincarnation process. It was like going down into the treacle - into the density. And that was really the end of the experience.

"I think I've included all the details, at least, the details that I've uncovered and I can remember. Actually, I only got this in the regression I did in 1994, twenty years after. I put in a lot of effort. I realized, golly, it's twenty years, so I decided I'd make an effort to try and get it."

The following NDE testimony comes from a Non-Gay NDEr: Carmel Bell's life story is a little different than most. Having survived four near-death experiences including one that lasted some 47 minutes following a cardiac arrest, her complete and total recovery still shocks people to this day. Her experiences equipped her with the unique skills of a Medical

Intuitive that, after twenty-five years of private practice, are now being extended to anyone through Bell's new book. "When All Else Fails" is the extraordinary story of how Carmel first discovered, and was gifted, energy by the Archangel Metatron during a near-death experience aged four. With great compassion, integrity and humor, she shares the story of how she has worked to heal herself and others using this energetic frequency for the last 25 years.

In February 2009 Carmel Bell suffered a cardiac arrest and died for 47 minutes. She was placed in a coma for four days and then spent six weeks in intensive care. The medical prognosis was she would be dependent on care all her life. Concerning the time she was dead she says, "I woke up out of my physical body immediately after my cardiac arrest, and realized I was dead. I was completely aware of my body lying on the bed, and of paramedics working on me. Simultaneously, I was also aware of heaven and of speaking to Jesus. In [my] book, I want to tell the story of my conversation with Jesus. I also want to introduce readers to life energy, and to Metatronic Level Energy -- the energy I used to heal myself."

While she was out of her body, she hovered like a ghost shuttling back and forth between Heaven and her bedroom to check what was happening with her body. In a coma for four days and in intensive care for six weeks, Carmel called in Metatronic Energy to heal her damaged brain and has now made a full recovery; one that has been hailed a medical miracle.

The following is Carmel's descriptions of her numerous NDEs.

I will talk first about my first experience of an NDE at four years of age. I consider there to be two types of NDE. The first type is where you are NOT meant to be dead and as a result, there is a lot of this type recorded and written about.

Type2 is where you are meant to be dead and you have asked to come back for your own reasons. They come across as very different experiences. I have had both types. Type 1 at four years old and type 2 at 47. I am alive because I insisted.

At four years of age, I awoke one morning very early and decided to help my mother by cleaning her sunroom. It was very cold so I was dressed in a winter nightgown and I turned on the little bar radiator in the sunroom to keep warm. I also had a scarf tied around my head to keep my hair out of my eyes. I bent over the radiator to dust the table and as I did my nightgown swung into it. The nightgown caught fire very rapidly, burning up my body. I did not notice the fire for a few moments, but when I did, I started to run, in a panic. It was about 5.30 in the morning, of a very cold winter morning. I thought that I was screaming but I was not, apparently. For some reason my father woke up. He does not know what woke him. He saw a light in the hallway, flickering. He thought about it for a while and decided not to worry, rolling over to go back to sleep until he realized that the light was FLICKERING. He says he jumped out of bed and ran to find me lying in the hallway ablaze. He began to beat the flames out with his hand screaming for my mother to come help.

Once I felt my father helping me, I died. I remember suddenly being surrounded by this intense light. It felt like a tunnel but all I could see was light almost so bright that I could not keep my eyes open. I felt/heard a rumbling noise and I walked towards that noise. Suddenly I was in a place that had a palm tree to the left of me and in front of me were these gates that were about 50ft wide and about 12ft high. These gates were silver and were made up of the images of all the animals on earth, and all the plants. They were alive and moving around together. These gates are still the most beautiful things I have ever seen.

There was a man waiting by the tree, not speaking, just watching me, and waiting for me to notice him. I was still 'in the light'. It made the ground look like a cloud but it felt solid. I knew there was more in this place but all I could see through the light were the gates, this man and the tree.

I walked up to the man and said 'Hello'. My voice echoed. He smiled at me and held out a hand. It was the hand of a workman. I took his hand but I have no recall of warmth, then he hugged me and walked me over to the tree where we sat. He started to talk, explaining that he was Jesus, my great grandfather, that I was there by accident, and that I needed to go back. I asked him what for and he told me that I had a big job to do for them all. He also told me that my future husband was waiting for me to help me. I asked what his name was and he told me 'his name is Bernie,' then together we walked back to my home and Jesus waited while I stepped back into my body. Then there was blinding pain and nothing.

I spent the next 43 years regretting being here and wishing to be home. I met Bernie, and we married, thank Source for that! He is truly a reward and a soulmate, which was confirmed when I died the second time.

14

CHANGES IN INTELLIGENCE QUOTIENT

Question #14 of our survey is for the surveyee to answer "yes" or "no" to the question of "Did your I.Q. change after your NDE?"

I.Q. refers to "Intelligence Quotient" which you can read more about in this Wikipedia article:

https://en.wikipedia.org/wiki/Intelligence_quotient

One possible NDE aftereffect is an increase in I.Q. In Debra Diamond's book, "Life After Near Death: Miraculous Stories of Healing and Transformation in the Extraordinary Lives of People With Newfound Powers," she profiles a dozen cases of specific cognitive and physiological near-death aftereffects, including: (1) elevated I.Q.; (2) newfound musical and artistic talents; (3) mathematical gifts; (4) enhanced hearing; (5) improved eyesight; (6) spontaneous healing; (7) electrical sensitivity.

Question #14 Statistics

Of the 41 Non-Gay NDErs: 21 Answered "Yes"; 20 Answered "No"
Of the 25 Gay NDErs: 14 Answered "Yes"; 11 Answered "No"

Chi-Square = 0.142489; p = 0.7058 > 0.05

Conclusion: Gay NDErs are not statistically more likely to have an I.Q. change after their NDE than Non-Gay NDErs.

Sample NDEs

The following NDE testimony comes from a Non-Gay NDEr: Martha Anne St. Claire, M.A., (formerly Martha A. Cassandra Musgrave) is a near-death experiencer, gerontologist, counselor, educator, writer, angelic messenger, spiritual medium, energetic healer, and pet communicator. In addition, she is also a near-death experience speaker who has been globally active, since her last near-death experience, in 1974. She offers individual sessions and group events that nourish and facilitate personal and planetary healing and transformation. Martha's down-to-earth, informative presentations have been enjoyed nation-wide, before multi-cultural audiences, through various organizations, at bookstores, churches, centers, expos, and fairs. She has served on the International Association for Near-Death Studies (IANDS) Board of Directors (2001-2003), working as the Friends of IANDS (FOI) International Chapter Coordinator. Her NDE research was published in (IANDS), The Journal of Near-Death Studies (Volume 15, No. 3, Spring, 1997).

Martha Anne St. Claire lives in northern California where she had a profound NDE when she was twenty-three years old that changed her life and provided a prophetic glimpse into our planetary future. She also was born premature, nearly dying at birth, and she also had an experience at age seven. However, the experience described below was the most profound, as she recalls.

In 1974, while water-skiing with friends, it was her last run for the day. The waves were choppy and so rough that she was forced to let go of the tow rope. As she fell, the triangle piece of the tow rope wrapped around her left forearm, jerking her down harshly and dragging her behind the boat, just under the surface of the water. Her boyfriend was driving the boat, chatting and drinking beer with his friend who was supposed to be watching but wasn't. They didn't notice that Martha had fallen down. As she struggled to hold her breath, she felt her spirit rise out of her body and then could see her body just under the surface of the water, being dragged at high speed. She saw her two friends in the boat talking to each other, oblivious to what was happening to her. She also saw her four-year old son playing on the shore with other friends. Martha's spirit traveled into a dark tunnel where she could hear loud clicking sounds. She traveled fast toward the light at the other end, excited, feeling she was going someplace she had once been. She came out where there were flowers everywhere, brightly colored and gorgeous. She then found herself in the universe surrounded by brilliant stars and planets all around her and into infinity. Although she couldn't see anything solid beneath her feet, she felt like she was standing on something and that she was home.

Martha's encounter with Melchizedek: [Note: Melchizedek was the king of Salem and priest of El Elyon ("God most high") who is mentioned twice in the Hebrew Bible. In Genesis 14:18-20, Melchizedek brings out bread and wine and blesses Abram. In Psalm 110:4, David references the Messiah as being "a priest forever, in the order of Melchizedek." In the Christian New Testament (Hebrews 5: 6-10, Hebrews 6: 20 and Hebrews 7: 1-21), Jesus Christ is identified as "a priest forever in the order of Melchizedek" quoting from Psalm 110:4. As such, Jesus assumes the role of High Priest once and for all.]

Suddenly, Martha found herself before Melchizedek. He didn't identify himself, but she recognized him and knew she had always known him. In the beautiful light that seemed like "liquid divine love", Martha experienced her true self, her full soul essence. "I felt free. It was wonderful seeing him! There are no words to describe my heavenly experience."

Melchizedek was bearded, stood eight or nine feet tall, wearing colors of forest green, rich burgundy, and gold on his velvet robe with a scarf covering his head and forehead. They communicated through thoughts. He said, "Are you ready to come?"

She exclaimed, "Already?" She felt that she had made a previous contract or agreement about her coming to earth and that he was aware of it. She knew it wasn't her time to die, that she hadn't accomplished all she had committed to do. She understood that souls on Earth had chosen Earth, their parents, the time to be here, lessons to be learned, and unique situations that was designed for each person's growth. She gained the understanding that we are not victims in the way we think we are; however, it takes great courage to be born on Earth, especially during this time. Above all, she knew we were given free choice.

Although Melchizedek let her know that she could stay in heaven and not return to earth, she panicked at the idea feeling like she had failed in some ways. She could see that there was more to do for her soul growth, helping others, and for her son. Melchizedek felt she was being too hard on herself.

She insisted that she wanted to go back. Then she was drawn toward a border that would lead her even more deeply into heaven, but knew if she passed through it, she couldn't return to Earth. She saw many other things, including in the distance, an entrance to a cave glowing with light that led into another dimension where people were studying and learning lots of information.

Concerning that dimension she states, "In that space you know all and have access to the mysteries of the universe and more." In another direction, she saw crystal-like buildings and temples with golden edges.

She saw that Earth was a difficult place to be, but there was a divine plan, and things would eventually be better. A twenty-year span between 1992 to 2012 was a time of great transition of the Earth in preparation for the dawning of the Millennium.

She understood that Mother Earth is alive and that surges of light are sent down to help heal her because she suffers from the pollution she is exposed to and also that the increments of light cause bizarre weather patterns, even if great transformation. She saw more frequent earthquakes, large tidal waves, a polar shift, and the ice caps breaking up and melting. She saw the Earth's surface changing, and many people dying, often in large numbers because they couldn't handle the intensity of vibration and its consequences and they chose to do die because their souls needed further growth in another sphere. In some cases, she saw people who had prepared themselves spiritually, were protected, while those around them died. However, she also saw that each soul chooses the time of death She saw three days of darkness. She also understood that certain catastrophes could be lessened or delayed through the power of prayer.

She says we have spiritual amnesia, having forgotten the knowledge we possessed before birth; there is a higher consciousness for each of us and it is important that we connect with God through prayer and meditation to be awakened in our souls.

Melchizedek showed Martha what would happen if she chose to die. She saw the boat being stopped and her body being carried to shore where she was given mouth-to-mouth resuscitation without success. Her boyfriend was crying and she knew he would feel guilty for the rest of his life. She saw her son and knew she couldn't leave him yet. She didn't want certain others to suffer because of her untimely death and because she had spiritual work to do, she chose to return to Earth, even if she so wanted to stay in the wonderful light.

Martha found herself back in her body which had a will of its own, feeling stunned and weak in the river. Coughing and sputtering, she surfaced a distance from the stopped boat, and tried to yell, "Don't you see, I'm drowning out here?!" Yet, even with the rope deeply meshed in her injured arm, she was in a state of utter bliss and transformation.

As they reached shore, her son said, "What took you so long, Mommy? I thought you were never coming back." She knew that somehow he was aware of more than her brief boat trip on the Sacramento River Delta. (This is a condensed version of Martha's NDE).

After her NDE, Martha's entire life changed and the blissful energy stayed with her for some time. Martha could see auras around others and in nature. Spiritual gifts, she'd had in childhood, opened to her even more. She didn't talk much about it because others were uncomfortable with her story or didn't understand. This was before the term "near-death experience" had even become known.

The longing to share the divine spirit she experienced during her NDE, led her, in the years that followed, on an inner journey of spiritual practice that included ministerial training through the Unity Church and a private counseling practice as a spiritual medium, angelic messenger, and energetic healer for humans and animals.

Martha's NDE vision of the future: Martha Anne St. Claire described her NDE visions of the future in the NBC television documentary entitled "Ancient Prophecies III." Here is how she described them:

"Basically, I saw that there was a 20-year period from 1992 to 2012. Things will be greatly accelerated on Earth. All these things will be manifest by great Earth changes: earthquakes, floods, tidal waves, great winds. I also saw there were certain areas that would be particularly affected - the areas of the east coast, which will be a surprised regarding earthquakes. (Martha also saw cement rubble in NYC and now wonders if she was seeing the events of 9/11.) I remember very clearly Japan slipping into the ocean. I was shown there was going to be something akin to three days of darkness. I don't feel it is from nuclear war. To me, it was more of a feeling of natural Earth disasters with smoke from volcanoes that would block the sun. We are all going to be on a roller-coaster ride, and yet, it is not forever. If we have darkness, it will pass. We will always have great light."

The following testimony comes from a Non-Gay person resulting from an attempted murder: It was the summer of 1978. I was traveling through the Southwest as a jewelry and giftware salesman, selling a wide range of items from Austrian crystals to feather earrings. On the way to Los Angeles from Las Vegas, I stopped to help a motorist whose car had broken down in the Mojave Desert. He was down on his luck, had no plans and nowhere to go, so I let him travel with me.

His name was Ray, and he looked to be in his early twenties. He was small, muscular, wiry, and slightly gaunt, as if underfed. I felt sorry for him, and in the three days we were together, I grew to trust him. I even started sending him on errands while I visited stores to sell my wares. At one point,

I gave him some of my clothes, and it pleased him to have something new to wear. He seemed calm and mostly satisfied.

The third night, we were camped out near Puddingstone Reservoir east of Claremont. I was sitting on the floor in the back of the large van, moving things around in the cupboards to make more room for the clothes, books, food, sample boxes, and my passenger's duffel bag and travel gear.

There was a loud explosion, and I felt a sharp, searing blow to the top of my head. Had the gas stove exploded? I looked up, but it was intact. Then I looked at Ray, sitting in the driver's seat, and I saw the black gun in his hand. His arm was resting on the back of the seat, aiming the pistol at my face. A bullet had hit me! At first, I thought he was warning me - that he was going to rob me. That suddenly seemed fine. Take it all, I thought. Take it all. Just leave me outside and drive away.

Another explosion shook me, and my ears rang with a terrible, high-pitched whine. I felt blood dripping down my face and the top of my head throbbed. He's not warning me, I realized. He's going to kill me. I am going to die.

There was no place to hide. I was stuck in an uncomfortable position surrounded by cabinets. There was nothing I could do. I heard myself whisper "Relax. It's out of your control. Breathe. Stay awake." My thoughts turned to death, and to God. "Thy will, not my will, be done." I let my body go, and I started to relax, to slump back. I watched my breath, in and out, in and out, in and out.

I began preparing for my death. I asked to be forgiven by anyone I had hurt and offered my forgiveness to everyone who had hurt me throughout my life. It was a full-color fast-reverse movie reel of my entire twenty-six years. I thought about my parents, my brothers and sisters, my lovers, my friends. I said goodbye. I said, "I love you."

Another explosion shook the van, and my body pulsed. I was not hit. The bullet missed me by a fraction of an inch, penetrating the cupboard I was leaning against. I relaxed back into my reverie. My luck could not hold out. Three bullets to go, if it was a revolver. I could only hope that the gun wasn't a semi-automatic.

Nothing mattered anymore but to be at peace. My van, my money, my business, my knowledge, my personal history, my freedom - all became worthless, meaningless, so much dust in the wind.

All I had of value was my body and my life, and that was soon to be gone. My attention was focused on the spark of light I called my Self, and my consciousness began to expand outward, extending my awareness in space and time. I heard my instructions clearly: Stay awake and keep breathing.

I prayed to my God, to the Great Spirit, to receive me with open arms. Love and light flowed through me, spreading out like a lighthouse beam, illuminating everything around me. The light grew inside me, and I expanded like a huge balloon until the van and its contents seemed small. A sense of peace and acceptance filled me. I knew I was close to leaving my body. I could sense the timeline of my life, both backward and forward. I saw the next bullet, a short distance into the future, leave the gun, jet toward my left temple, and exit with brains and blood on the right side of my head. I was filled with awe. To see life from this expanded perspective was like looking down into a dollhouse, seeing all the rooms at once, all the detail, so real and so unreal at the same time. I looked into the warm and welcoming golden light with calm and acceptance.

The fourth explosion shattered the silence, and my head was pushed violently to the side. The ringing in my ears was deafening. Warm blood rushed down my head and onto my arms and thighs, dripping onto the floor. But strangely, I found myself back in my body, not out of it. Still surrounded by light, love, and peace, I began looking inside my skull, trying to find the holes. Perhaps I could see light through them? I did a quick check of my feelings, abilities, thoughts, and sensations, looking for what might be missing. Surely the bullet had affected me. My head was throbbing, but I felt strangely normal.

I decided to look at my assassin, to look death in the face. I picked up my head and turned my eyes toward him. He was shocked. Jumping up from his seat, he shouted, "Why aren't you dead, man? You're supposed to be dead!"

"Here I am." I said quietly.

"That's too weird! It's just like my dream this morning! I kept shooting at him, but he wouldn't die! But it wasn't you in the dream, it was somebody else!"

This was very strange. Who was writing this script? I wondered. I began to speak slowly and calmly, trying to settle him down. If I could get him talking, I thought, maybe he wouldn't shoot again. He kept yelling, "Shut up! Just shut up!" as he peered out the windows into the darkness. He nervously walked closer to me, gun in hand, examining my bloody head, trying to understand why the four bullets he had pumped into me hadn't finished me off.

I could still feel blood oozing down my face and could hear it dripping onto my shoulder. Ray said, "I don't know why you aren't dead, man. I shot you four times!"

"Maybe I'm not supposed to die," I said calmly.

"Yeah, but I shot you!" he said, with disappointment and confusion in his voice. "I don't know what to do."

"What do you want to do?" I asked.

"I wanted to kill you, man, to take this van and drive away. Now I don't know." He seemed worried, uncertain. He was beginning to slow down, becoming less jumpy.

"Why did you want to kill me?"

"Because you had everything, and I had nothing. And I was tired of having nothing. This was my chance to have it all." He was still pacing back and forth in the van, looking out the windows at the black night outside.

"What do you want to do now?" I asked.

"I don't know, man," he complained. "Maybe I should take you to the hospital."

My heart leapt at this chance, this opportunity - a way out. "Okay," I said, not wanting to make him feel out of control. I wanted it to be his idea, not mine. I knew that his anger sprang from feeling out of control, and I didn't want to make him feel angry.

"Why were you so nice to me, man?"

"Because you're a person, Ray."

"But I wanted to kill you! I kept taking out my gun and pointing it at you, when you were asleep or not looking. But you were being so nice to me, I couldn't do it."

My time sense was altered. I realized that I had no idea how long it had been since the first bullet. After what felt like many minutes, Ray came up to me, still in my crouched, locked-in position, and said, "Okay, man, I'm going to take you to a hospital. But I don't want you to move, so I'm going to put some stuff on you so you can't move, okay?"

Now he was asking my permission. "Okay," I said softly. He began taking various boxes filled with samples and stacked them around me. "Are you okay?" he asked.

"Yeah, I'm okay. A little uncomfortable, but it's all right."

"All right, man. I'm going to take you to a hospital I know of. Now don't move. And don't die on me, okay?"

"Okay," I promised. I knew I wouldn't die. This light, this power inside me was so strong, so certain. Each breath felt like my first, not my last. I was going to survive. I knew it. Ray lowered the pop-top of the van, secured the straps, and started up the engine. I could feel the van backing up on the dirt road, finding the pavement and moving forward to my freedom.

He drove on and on - to where, I had no idea. Were we bound for a hospital, as he said, or toward some horrible fate? If he was capable of killing me with a gun, he was capable of lying, or worse. How did he know where to go? We were in Claremont. Los Angeles was over an hour away. I used that hour to re-play the scenes and analyze the past three days, trying to understand what had happened, and why.

Eventually, I felt the van slow, pull over and stop. The engine was turned off. Silence filled the space. I waited. It was still dark outside. We had not pulled into a driveway. There were no lights. This was not a hospital. Ray walked back toward me with his gun in his hand. He pulled away one of the boxes and sat down on the foam bed, facing me. He looked distraught, head hanging down. His words cut deep through my cloud of hope. "I have to kill you, man," he said calmly.

"Why?" I asked quietly.

"If I take you to the hospital, they'll put me back in jail. I can't go back to jail, man. I can't."

"They wouldn't put you in jail if you take me to the hospital," I said slowly, still feigning injury, passivity. I knew that I might find an opening, a moment when I could surprise him, overpower him, take away his gun. As long as he didn't know I was okay, I had an advantage.

"Oh yes they would, man. They'd know I shot you, and they'd lock me up."

"We don't have to tell them. I won't tell them."

"I can't trust you, man. I wish I could, but I can't. I can't go back to jail, that's all. I have to kill you." He seemed forlorn. This was not where he wanted to be. He wasn't making any moves. His gun hung limply from his hand, pointed down toward the floor. The boxes were still stacked around me. I couldn't judge how much strength I had, whether it would be enough to push out and wrestle him down. He was small but strong. Was he still full of adrenaline? That would make him even stronger. My strength lay in words, in verbal swordplay. If I could keep him talking, he wouldn't take stronger action.

"Maybe I could go into the hospital alone, Ray. You wouldn't even have to be there. You could get away."

"No, man," he said, shaking his head." As soon as you told them, they'd come find me. They'd track me down."

I was silent. That didn't work, I thought.

He said, "Why aren't you dead, man? I shot you four times in the head. How come you're still alive and talking? You should be dead! I know I didn't miss." He looked again at my head, taking it in one hand and turning it to the left and right. "Does it hurt?" he asked. He seemed genuinely concerned.

"Yeah, it hurts," I lied. "But I think I'm going to be okay."

"Well, I don't know what to do. I can't take you to the hospital. I can't just let you go, because you'll go to the police. Why were you so damn nice to me, man? No one's ever been that nice to me before. It made it harder to kill you. You kept buying me stuff, and giving me stuff. I just couldn't decide when to do it."

Not if, but when.

"What would you do with all this stuff if you had it, Ray?" I asked.

"I could go home and be somebody, I could do stuff. I'd have enough money to buy my way out of there, man." Ray began to talk. He talked about his home in East Los Angeles, the poverty around him, his anger, the schoolteachers who made him feel stupid, his father who drank too much and beat him, and being tough on the streets. He talked about joining the Army, how that was supposed to make it work, but he couldn't stand being told what to do all the time, so he went AWOL. He talked about dealing drugs, and drug deals going bad, and how he ripped off his dealer buddies. That's why he had to leave L.A., because they were looking for him. He talked about stealing his father's gun and money before he left, then he realized there was no place to hide, so he decided to turn back. Maybe he could do one more rip-off and get rich. He just needed one hit, one sucker. If his target was rich enough, he could pay off the dealers and start over. So he decided to kill whoever stopped. Whoever came by to help him. Me.

The night had turned to morning, the sky shifting slowly from indigo to blue. The sound of chirping birds made me grateful to be alive.

"I'm pretty stiff and sore, Ray, I'd feel better if I could get up and stretch." I was still in the same position I had been in for six hours. Dried blood was plastered to my hair and face, my shins hurt from being pushed against the edge of a cupboard door, and my back was stiff and throbbing.

"Okay, man, I'm going to let you up, but don't do anything stupid, okay?"

"Okay, Ray. You just tell me what to do and I'll do it."

Remind him that he is in control. Don't let him feel out of control. Look for an opening.

He moved the boxes from around me, stepped back with the gun in his hand, and opened the door. I crawled slowly out of the van, stretching upright for the first time. How beautiful the world was to my new eyes. Everything shone as if made of sparkling crystal.

We had stopped on a residential street near a small pond at the bottom of an embankment. He gestured down the dirt trail that led to the water. As I walked down the steep incline I thought, "Is this death again, tapping on my shoulder? Will he shoot me in the back and push me into the water?" I felt weak and vulnerable, yet simultaneously immortal and impervious to his bullets. I walked erect and unafraid. He followed me to the water's edge and stood by as I squatted down and rinsed my bloodied hands and face, splashing cool, fresh water on myself. I stood up slowly and faced Ray. He looked at me curiously.

"What would you do if I handed you this gun right now?" he asked, holding the gun out to me.

My answer was my first thought: "I'd throw it out into the water," I said.

"Aren't you mad at me, man?" he asked. He seemed incredulous.

"No, why should I be mad?"

"I shot you, man, you ought to be angry! I'd be f---g furious! You wouldn't want to kill me if I gave you this gun?"

"No, Ray, I wouldn't. Why should I? I have my life and you have yours."

"I don't understand you, man. You are really weird, really different than anyone I've ever met before. And I don't know why you didn't die when I shot you." Silence. Better left unanswered. As we stood at the water's edge, I realized that Ray had undergone as profound a transformation as I had. We were both different people than we had been the day before.

"What should we do now, Ray?"

"I don't know, man. I can't take you to the hospital. I can't let you go. I don't know what to do."

So we continued our talk, seeking a solution to his dilemma. We explored the possibilities - what could we agree to? I made suggestions, he told me why they wouldn't work. I made other suggestions. He listened, considered, rejected, and relented. We sought a compromise.

Ultimately, we found a bargain we could agree to: I would let him go, and he would let me go. I promised not to turn him in or report him to the police, but on one condition - he had to promise that he would never do anything like this again. He promised. What choice did he have?

As the sun was rising over the hills, we climbed back into the van. I sat in the passenger seat as he drove to a place that he knew. He parked, and I gave him all the cash I had, about $200, and a couple of watches I thought he could pawn. We walked together across the street. The sun was shining. t was early in the day but already warm. He had his Army jacket and sleeping bag under one arm, his duffel bag slung over his shoulder. Somewhere in the bundle there was a black gun.

We shook hands. I smiled at him, and he continued to look confused. Then I said goodbye and walked away.

In the emergency room of L.A. County Hospital, a doctor scraped away small bits of metal, skin and hair, and sewed stitches into my scalp. He asked me how it had happened, and I told him, "I was shot, four times."

"You're a lucky man," he said. "The two bullets that hit you both glanced off your skull. You have to report this to the police, you know."

"Yes, I know," I said. I already knew that I was lucky, but even more, I felt blessed. I didn't go to the police. I had made a promise and had received a promise in return. I kept my promise. I believe that Ray kept his.

15

PARANORMAL EXPERIENCES

Question #15 of our survey is for the surveyee to answer "yes" or "no" to the question of "Did you have any paranormal experiences (e.g. apparitions) since your NDE?"

For a complete list of paranormal experiences, see this Wikipedia article.

https://en.wikipedia.org/wiki/Category:Parapsychology

According to the IANDS.org website: (1) NDErs become quite intuitive after an NDE; (2) Psychic displays can be commonplace such as: (a) out-of-body experiences; (b) manifestation of "beings" met in near-death state; (c) "remembering" the future; (d) finishing another person's sentence; (e) "hearing" plants and animals "speak"; (3) These psychic displays are not only worrisome to family and friends, they can be frightening to them; (4) The NDEr's religious beliefs do not alter or prevent this amplification of psychic faculties and stimuli. Yet, experiencers willing to learn how to control and refine these abilities, consider them beneficial.

Question #15 Statistics

Of the 41 Non-Gay NDErs: 28 Answered "Yes"; 13 Answered "No"
Of the 25 Gay NDErs: 17 Answered "Yes"; 8 Answered "No"
Chi-Square = 0.00061324; p = 0.9802 > 0.05
Conclusion: Gay NDErs are not statistically more likely to have any paranormal experiences (e.g. apparitions) since their NDE than Non-Gay NDErs.

Sample NDEs

The following NDE comes from a Non-Gay NDEr: Introduction to Donna's NDE: Donna Gatti is the owner of Angel Academy (www. angelacademy.com), a website devoted to angel lovers, the study of spirituality, and the attainment of enlightenment. She is also the author of the books Angels and Alchemy and When Angels Speak. Her stated goal is to connect people with their guardian angel and spiritual guides. As a translator for these heavenly beings, she delivers personal messages, word for word, from beyond the veil. She describes what is called "The Angel's Guarantee of Love, Honor, and Truth:

LOVE: You cannot imagine the depth and magnitude of your angels' love. They smile upon you as they observe the good things that you do. When you make a mistake, they encourage you to get up and keep going. They shower you with loving thoughts and gentle feelings as you struggle to overcome the difficulties of daily living. Always they are at your side, these faithful and wise companions. In the morning, your guardians greet you with warm enthusiasm, thrilled for another new day of serving you. At night, they stroke your brow with tender affection, as you are serenely cherished. There is nothing on Earth that can compare to the power of an angel's openhearted love.

HONOR: Angels honor you for simply being you. There are no rules in the spiritual realm other than "to be." Therefore, angels do not judge, condemn or criticize. You do not have to say or do anything at all to be worthy to receive. Angels respect you for the brilliant light that shines forth from your soul. You deserve honor because you possess a noble spirit. As a child of the Creator, you are spiritual royalty.

TRUTH: Telling someone the truth is an act of love. Your angels want you to know what is true and what is not. As the veil of illusion is lifted, you will see yourself and others differently. When you view the world as it really is, pain and suffering leave you. Grief and sadness dissolve into a greater understanding. Peace of mind comes to those who strive for truth.

Donna Gatti's NDE and the wonderful insights she learned: Within each of us dwells a mystic, a powerful source of spiritual energy and divine intelligence. This brilliant light inside your soul longs to be set free, to shine and radiate magic in your life. Allow it to come forth and rejuvenate you. As the angels refresh your memories of Home, you will recall why you were born and what you are here to do. You are a child of God, the Creator of the Universe, and you have certain unalienable rights. Step forward and claim your inheritance.

My clients have experienced the joy of communicating with their angels; they have felt the love that exists only in the hidden realms. At this precious moment in time, I have been given permission to perform this sacred work. Many others have learned the names of their angels and received heavenly guidance. You can too. The world is changing. Soon, everybody will be in direct communication with his or her angels and guides.

My angels have granted all of my requests, and your angels can do the same for you. I am deeply indebted to these marvelous beings of light, and they have asked me to do only one thing in return:

"Bring humankind nearer to us. We wish to come closer to them, but their fears place us at a distance. One tiny step towards our dimension gives us the permission we need to work miracles in their lives. We long to embrace them with love; we yearn to guide them and whisper into their mind's ear the words they need to hear. We pray for them, yet they cannot hear our prayers. They feel desolate and alone. It is now time for angels and humanity to come together, to join hands with one another, and to create Heaven on Earth."

My first encounter with angels occurred in 1974. While undergoing a surgical procedure, the doctor made a mistake, cut an artery, and I lost too much blood to sustain life. As my physical body lay dying on the operating table, I rose up and surveyed the situation. I noticed that the doctors and nurses were upset, and were working desperately to save me. In my ethereal body, with my mental faculties and personality intact, I went nose-to-nose with each one and told them to relax, that I was okay, but they ignored me. Frustrated, I moved higher up, away from my body, and began to fly. Gravity had no effect on me. Flying was natural and effortless, sort of like swimming underwater, but in an ocean of brilliant white light.

During my near-death experience, two Escort Angels came to take me Home. Since then, I have been in touch with the celestial realm. I have seen angels as big as skyscrapers and others as small as a pinpoint of light. Archangel Michael, the Buddha, White Eagle, Warrior Angels, sepia-colored cherubs, and dancing light beings have shown themselves to me. I have entered the Halls of Knowledge and received instructions from the Great White Brotherhood, an organization on the ethereal plane that is dedicated to the spiritual evolution of humanity. There is no discrimination of any kind on the Other Side. "Great" and "White" refer to the loving white light in the higher dimensions. As no one is above or below another, what one can do all can do. I have seen, and you can too.

I heard a kind and gentle voice speak. Without my asking, the Voice answered all the big questions about life. Then, my smallest concerns were addressed as if they were matters of great importance. When the Voice told me why Aunt Bettie married Uncle Fred, I giggled with joy and contentment. My curiosity had been completely satisfied, and I felt like a child held in the arms of a loving parent after a hard day at school. The Voice in the Light had anticipated and joyfully fulfilled my needs and desires, with good humor, extreme love and enormous tenderness.

The nurse yelled, "We're losing her," and at the sound of distress I was propelled upward. The farther up I went, the brighter the Light became. Two cherubs appeared, one on either side of me, and we slowly drifted to the corner of the ceiling. We communicated through mental telepathy, which is faster and more efficient than mere words. They told me they were Escort Angels and had come to take me Home. But before we could go, I had to look at the body I was leaving behind. She was twenty-five years old and in perfect health, except for the loss of blood and spirit. I determined that the situation was not serious enough, and in less than an instant I reentered my physical body through the navel. I was back on Earth and suffering from Homesickness.

I looked up at the ceiling to see the Escort Angels fly through the wall, and I became emotionally distraught. I was embarrassed because I had forgotten to thank them for coming to get me. Years later, whenever I thought about my lack of good manners, I cringed inside. One day, I heard one of them say, "Why don't you thank us now?" I laughed, relieved that I could right a wrong. I said, "Thank you," and I saw balloons, confetti, and two tiny cherubs dancing in celebration.

Donna Gatti's reincarnation experiences: At the age of four, I suddenly recalled my prior lives. Time stood still as I watched my mother on her hands and knees scrubbing the kitchen floor. The walls and ceiling dissolved into nothingness, and the roof disappeared from our house. A physical sensation came over me, as if an unseen force had placed a Cloak of Protection around my shoulders. Mother's words could not be heard above that peculiar rushing sound of the ethereal silence. My spiritual eyes witnessed a substance, which looked like grains of black sand, being poured into the crown of my head. At that precise moment, I saw a long line of women who had been my mothers in previous lifetimes. And I knew, with that strange and wonderful sense of knowingness, that I was not a helpless child but a powerful spiritual being on an extended journey, a long way from Home.

A similar episode occurred when I was fifteen. Fighting in Vietnam had just begun and our boys were going off to war. As my girlfriends discussed the situation, I found myself outside of present time. I was transported to airspace over a battlefield, looking down at the bloody carnage. I was one of the dead soldiers wearing an American Civil War uniform. I recalled rising up, out of the confines of my physical body. But before I (my ethereal body) could leave the Earth's atmosphere, I had to view the scene below. There was a lesson to be learned, and it would reveal itself to me only if I looked to find it.

While gazing at the wounded young man's body, which I had inhabited only seconds ago, I made a vow. I promised myself that I would never again participate in a war. To lose precious life in a fight against my fellow man, a war declared by men who did not shed a drop of their own blood, was stupid and senseless. I vowed to find another way. Since then, I have reincarnated over and over again, but always as a woman.

I work for the angels. They give me a specific job to do and all the help I need to complete it. My first project was to act as scribe for "When Angels Speak: Messages from the Keepers of The Lion's Gate," which I co-authored with Nadira Duran. It is available in paperback at our bookstore.

"Angels and Alchemy" is the title of my second book, which was published in the summer of 2003. An e-book version will be out very soon. If you love angels and want to know more about what they do and how they do it, this is the right book for you. Written in novel form, "Angels and Alchemy" is based on ancient wisdom and spiritual truths. The story reveals secrets nobody knows unless he or she has actually seen and conversed with heavenly beings.

The angels made me their writer, even though I did not go to college and hold no professional degrees of any kind. Universities cannot prepare a person to do spiritual work. My credentials are mystical experiences and encounters with angels. I've been to the Other Side on many occasions and have learned the language of Spirit. It is important to know that extraordinary things can and do happen to ordinary people like me. When you know that such wonders actually exist, then you begin to dream of having your own. You can have what you want and everything you need. All is within the realm of possibility. First one, and then another, until everyone has the ability to travel with ease beyond the veil.

My current task is connecting people with their angels and spiritual guides. I walk the bridge between Heaven and Earth, in search of spiritual nourishment. The angels have asked me to step forward and hold my lamp high, so that those who seek can find their way.

The following NDE comes from a Non-Gay NDEr: FEBRUARY 15th 2009 3:15 am. I awoke for no known reason and lay still for a few seconds, wondering what was wrong, as I reoriented myself and sat up. I realized straight away that something was wrong, so I turned around and looked. Although it was the middle of the night and dark, I could see perfectly well. The first thing I noticed was that I was looking at my body. The second thing I noticed was that it was as if I was staring at someone else's body. I had no real feeling towards it, which now I think is strange.

I quickly realized that I was dead. I kept looking for the tunnel but none happened. I decided then that I did not want to be dead so I mustered my energy together as hard as I could and shook my husband yelling at him to wake up and help me. He did! But instead of helping me he went to the toilet, figuring that this was what woke him up; a busting bladder. I sat back and waited for him, conscious that every second made me deader. Bernie came back into the room and climbed into bed. He snuggled up to my body and realized almost straightaway that I was not breathing. He turned on the light. I watched his face register shock, horror and grief and then I knew I was in good hands. As soon as I realized that Bernie was looking after my body, I was in heaven. I think that heaven is all around us, in another dimension. I do not think that we go up or down, though we may. It just feels like another dimension.

The first thing I noticed was the same man was waiting for me, Jesus, but this time he was not alone, there were hundreds of people there. Moving about with what seemed to be purpose to me. It was dark, like this place was in space and I could see the tree again. There were no gates this time, but there was now a mountain that looked to be about 20kms away. On the top, there was a very large living Light presence. I knew that this was GOD or SOURCE and that this is why it is called the LIGHT. There were Angels there as well. The easiest way to differentiate them is that they had different energy, like they were lit from within and were not quite connected to us but were benevolent to us. They did not have wings but I could understand why they would be drawn that way.

Knowledge came in suddenly, from everywhere. The easiest way again to explain is that I was a computer user going into the main frame. My thoughts were much faster and much clearer. My IQ would have been doubled I believe. So not only could I think faster and clearer, I could tolerate knowing more and being told more at the same time. I was able to talk to Jesus and observe my body back on earth being worked on.

Jesus told me about his connection to me and told me that I had fulfilled my life job and that my reward was being called home. I felt relief and joy that I had been successful. My life has been spent caring for and genuinely helping people, often in the face of being ridiculed, ostracized and held apart. It was a very painful life and I was glad it was over. Then I thought of my husband who had come to earth to help me. How could I leave him? He needed my support as I needed his.

I began to argue with Jesus to be allowed to go back. I asked to speak to God. Metatron appeared then and explained to me that I could not speak directly to God, as it would annihilate my essence to do so.

While I was talking to Metatron, I was still seeing my body on earth. I was aware of the electric shocks (7 in total) as they happened as each jolted my spirit as well.

I was aware that my animals that had passed over were also in heaven. I played and talked with them for a while which was terrific.

Then I spoke to some nephews who had died when they were very young. I was happy to see that they had still grown up and were interested in their family although one of them was about to be reborn. I spoke to my grandparents. I also saw some of my past lives, with Jesus telling me about them as I viewed them.

All the time I was asking why I had died and could I now go back? It seemed that the Spiritual Beings felt I needed a rest and that Bernie would struggle but would come home to me soon enough. I just remember feeling angry that they could not really understand that he had been loyal to me and I should be loyal to him but NOW I believe that they were trying to get me to 100% agree to the next job they wanted me to do, which was bigger than the first. And much harder.

So there I was, flashing back and forth, watching the firemen, Bernie and the ambulance officers working on my body. Your brain capacity and your consciousness are so much greater in Spirit. You are capable of much more than you are when it all has to be housed in your human body. I became extremely aware that the body is completely a recording system for memories and events from not only this life, but past lives where there is unfinished business.

After a time I suddenly knew that if I did not go back, then I would not be able to go back. Jesus told me that now was the time to go if I was going. I only realized later that the plan must have been for me to come back, even though they told me that I was meant to stay. I think I was meant to be dead but they knew that the choice would be mine. They were very sad to see me 'go'. I waved goodbye to my Guides, hugged Jesus and viewed GOD/SOURCE again, hoping to remember what it was.

I know that a lot of 'information' was put into my brain for safekeeping so that I could not access it until my brain was healed again. Jesus told me that I would be fine, that my body would heal and I trusted him and his truth of the situation. He has been correct even though I was dead for so long and without oxygen except for emergency procedures.

I am now accessing the information that they put into me.

Anyway, Jesus told me that this would be the hardest thing I have ever done. He asked me to teach, to form groups of like-minded people. He told me that I would feel sorrow and betrayal but that I would be loved. I said goodbye and stepped back into my body. My feet entered first. I have had pain walking ever since. It is like walking on knives. I feel like the little mermaid.

I felt pain like I have never felt before. I saw a blinding flash of light.

The next thing I knew it was four days later and I could feel Bernie next to me. 'I came back for you' I croaked out as I dropped the energy that I use into my brain, telling it to heal. I did not have another conscious memory for nearly six weeks.

February 15, 2009 NDE 1: I had come home from a wedding earlier that evening and went to bed as per usual. I suddenly woke up and realized that something was wrong. I could not identify what exactly was wrong, but then I realized that as I moved my body, my body did not move. I sat up and my body stayed lying down on its back with the left arm thrown over my face. I knew then that I was dead but I did not feel any concern or panic about that.

My husband was asleep next to me so I started to yell at him 'Wake up! I'm dead!' and I gathered all my energy together to shake him as hard as I could. After a bit of time he woke up and I felt relieved but then he rolled out of bed and went to the toilet. I sat back and waited for his return. I felt very upset that he had left me instead of rescuing me.

He came back into the room and climbed into bed, touching me as he did and then he suddenly sat up, turned on the light and gently moved my arm off my face. I could see the grief come into his face, the horror, the shock. He rolled me over onto my side and opened my eyes, staring into them for a while, and then he sat up, pushed me back onto my back and started CPR. He also started yelling to one of our sons to come help, come call the ambulance.

I became aware that I was in another place, yet I still maintained an awareness of my body on the bed. It was blackness and night sky, a sense that there was ground beneath me. I sensed/felt/saw people all around me. One of them walked up to me and said hello as if I knew him. Suddenly I did. I had met this man before, when I died when I was four. 'Hello,' I said, 'Jesus?' I asked. He smiled.

'Yes.' I began to ask questions like 'Why are you here?' YOU as in Jesus. He explained that he was there as my father of my family tree, that I was his great x many granddaughter. He was not there as Jesus the Messiah, if that makes sense. There was a difference. He told me that I was meant to be dead, that I had fulfilled my task.

I argued with him about that. I wanted to go back to earth for my husband. I have children but I knew that they would be fine without me. My husband had come to earth in part for me. I could not abandon him now.

I spoke to some of my relatives and agreed to pass messages on for them. I spoke to my animals and agreed to help animals. I laughed, I cried. All the time I was also aware of my body and I was watching what was happening to it.

Finally, Jesus told me that if I was going back I had to go now or I would be too damaged. I stepped backwards to reenter 100%. He asked me if I would do a favor for them by carrying on the energy work I had been doing. I agreed. Then I was back in my body and I could feel an electric shock through my body. My heart started and my breathing started at once. [Carmel Bell's NDE ends here.]

Aftereffects: Ultimately, Carmel's story is one of hope because it shows the way to a realm of infinite possibilities for healing and recovery. She became a medical intuitive before it was fashionable; among her clients are medical practitioners who refer their patients to her. Carmel describes herself as a cartographer, reading the map of her client's bodies.

"Your story is written in every cell of your being. Every moment matters because everything you hear, think, feel, eat, read, see and do will be recorded somewhere in your body."

Under a facade of normalcy, many people hide sorrow, anger, disappointment and other corrosive emotions that don't show up on medical tests. So, in one sense, our medical professionals don't have the full story.

Carmel's abilities allow her see into the core of the illness and it's often not what's expected. She says, "Simply put, very few people are true to themselves. Their battle between their heart and what is expected of them, by themselves and by others, becomes overwhelming. They come to see me when all else has failed."

The following NDE comes from a Non-Gay NDEr: My near-death experience was due to the fact that somebody was trying to murder me. It turns out that my ex-boyfriend teamed up with the ex-wife of the new man I was dating. The new man I was dating did not tell me he was married, and when his then-wife found out, she freaked out and stalked me. She found out where my ex-boyfriend lives and they teamed up, along with several other people, to murder me on April 8th, 2006. My then four-year-old son was also in the house.

It was 4:51 a.m. when I felt myself leaving my body and hovering by the ceiling. It was exhilarating and peaceful, and I enjoyed the experience. I was simply an energy hovering above my body. I gravitated towards the opening of a tunnel just outside of my living room window. I was not ready to go into the tunnel, and as soon as I felt that way, I went right back in my body and jolted up in bed. Then I could hear two people at least outside my front door. They threw something at my front door that made a snap crackle pop sound. Like a firecracker that didn't detonate properly.

I knew as I was having the experience that is a near-death experience, but at that point I did not see a light. 24 hours later, when I woke up the next morning, a light appeared to me in my living room and told me the truth about my life. I learned some very difficult truths about my life, but God was very supportive, kind and caring. The light was beautiful. It looked like the Sun, but it didn't hurt to look at it. God was very happy that I quit my drug and alcohol Habit to be a good mother to my son, and he gave me an assignment, which is to make a movie about my life. God told me that the purpose of my life was at each 11 or respect, and because I quit drugs and alcohol to be a good mom, he would allow my dream to come true. Right now I'm finishing up a book which will be out spring of 2021. It tells the story how they plotted against me. My son also said that he experienced the sensation of being out of his body that night as well. I'm writing a book and hopes that it will become a film and we can make the movie. I know who the director and producer is going to be and I'm very excited about it! There's more to the story, but that's the gist of it.

16

CHANGES IN FEELINGS OF LOVE

Question #16 of our survey is for the surveyee to answer "yes" or "no" to the question of "Were there any changes in your feelings of compassion / caring / loving since your NDE?"

According to Dr. Bruce Greyson and Dr. Kenneth Ring's study into "Life Changes Inventory - Revised" changes in the NDErs concern for others includes: (1) an increased desire to help others; (2) more compassion for others; (3) an increase in the ability to listen patiently; (4) more tolerance for others; (5) increased sensitivity to the suffering of others; (6) an ability to express love for others openly; (7) a greater insight into the problems of others; (8) better understanding of others; (9) an increase in empathy with others; (10) a greater acceptance of others.

Question #16 Statistics

Of the 41 Non-Gay NDErs: 39 Answered "Yes"; 2 Answered "No"
Of the 25 Gay NDErs: 22 Answered "Yes"; 3 Answered "No"
Chi-Square = 1.12503; p = 0.2888 > 0.05

Conclusion: Gay NDErs are not statistically more likely to have any changes in their feelings of compassion / caring / loving since their NDE than Non-Gay NDErs.

Sample NDEs

The following NDE testimony comes from a Non-Gay NDEr: In early summer of 1979, David Oakford (www.soulbared.com) was 19-years old and having problems dealing with his life situation. His childhood was not designed to enable him to properly deal with life in general. He had no self-esteem and everything he did to find peace within just did not work. He was pretty miserable then and felt lost and unloved. He turned to drugs and alcohol. He needed to find the peace within himself and he felt it calling him. It was at a party that David had an overdose of drugs and had a near-death experience. His near-death experience is one of the most profound you will ever read. The following is his near-death experience testimony which also appears in Kevin Williams' book Nothing Better Than Death. A more detailed edition of David Oakford's wonderful testimony is published in his book Soul Bared: A Metaphysical Journey which I highly recommend.

David's date with destiny: I laid down to use the stability of the Earth in an effort to maintain a hold on reality. I knew I had to do that in order to be able to come back down.

The next thing I knew I was riding in my friend's car. I thought we went up north, crossed the Mackinaw Bridge and came back again. We rode past my childhood home and I saw my parents sitting on the porch.

I felt drawn to the trees. I could see and feel their strength. I saw their roots going deep into the ground. I mean I actually saw the tree roots physically reaching below the ground. I told my friends about the car ride after the experience and they told me that the only place I went was to the chair they carried me to after I passed out on the porch.

I did wake up in the chair my friends say they put me in a bit later. When I woke up I could feel the organs in my body working, each one separately as well as all together. I could not see my friends anywhere. I could see in all the rooms of the house at the same time. The stereo was playing the Doors "Absolutely Live" album, except the volume was way too loud for me. Since I did not see any of my friends around I got up and tried to turn the music down, but could not. No matter what I did the music kept playing. I knew the stereo too. I had a real problem with the noise. It was tearing at me and I could not figure out why nor could I adjust the volume.

I called out to my friends and nobody came. I tried to unplug the stereo but that did not work either. Every time I tried to touch the cord to unplug it I could not grasp it. It just kept on playing "LA Woman" and the sound rattled my very being.

I ran all over the house calling for my friends, yelling repeatedly that the music was too loud but I was not heard. I pleaded for the music to be turned down. I tried to go outside but I could not feel the doorknob. I could see the daylight outside but could not go outside. I ended up hiding in the bathroom in an unsuccessful attempt to escape the noise. I looked in the mirror and could not see myself. That frightened me greatly.

I went back into the family room and saw my body sitting in the chair. It looked like I was sleeping. I wondered how I could be looking at myself. I got a bit scared then because I could see me from outside of me, from all different angles except from the inside angle I was used to seeing myself.

I was alone. I was confused and very scared. I tried to get back into my body but could not. I could not touch the ground either. I was floating. I rose up into a spot above my body and kind of just hung there. I could no longer move. I called out for help and nobody came. I tried to go out the door but like the stereo I could not touch the doorknob. I was scared and alone and did not know what to do. I did not understand what was happening to me.

I asked God to help me. I did believe in God then, but I was kind of angry at him because of the crappy life I was experiencing. I reasoned that if God were really the omnipotent and omniscient being I was taught he was he would not have let me experience the pain I had experienced throughout my life. I thought that if there was a time I needed God, it was now! I was not disappointed with the result of my plea for help.

I looked over by the door to the outside and saw a beautiful being standing there. His feet did not touch the floor. His feet just blended into thin air. He looked both female and male and was young. I could not tell his/her sex. His hair was curly and he was about my height. He had this glow about him too. The glow was green close to him, then blue, then pure white in the upper areas. He said, "I am here to help you" but when he spoke his mouth did not move. I did not actually hear him speak with my ears. I felt what he was saying.

When I saw this being and he spoke to me, I was no longer afraid. I actually felt peace and comfort like I had never felt before. I felt the peace I was searching for throughout my entire life. The feeling was very familiar to me, like I had felt it before but not in this life.

This wonderful being called me by a name I do not remember. I told him he must have the wrong guy and that the name he used for me was not my name. He laughed and said that I was a great "master" and that I had just forgotten who I was. I did not believe him, because I did not really know for sure what a "master" was then and if I were this great master I would not have had all the problems I had. I felt that I was an evil being because that is what I was told in my life several times by many.

He told me his name, but I do not remember it. He told me that he had been with me always and told me that he knew that I had a very hard life and that he would help me understand why if I really wanted to. He told me that he would help me remember who I am. He said that he would understand if I did not believe him and offered to prove to me that he knew everything about me.

He told me things that I did when I as a child that proved to me that he was always with me. He told me about things I had only thought about. He told me that I could go anywhere I wanted to go and that he would show me how to do it if I wanted him to. He said that if I needed to come back and see my body I could. My body would be fine because I was still connected to it somehow.

When we spoke to each other we did so telepathically. The expression on his face was a happy one all the time.

I told him that I would like to see the pyramids in Egypt as well as the southwest United States. He told me that all I had to do was trust him, think about where I wanted to go, and we would go. I thought about the pyramids and we were there in an instant. I do not know why I chose the pyramids, the thought just popped into me so I went with that. While we were there he told me some things about the pyramids and Egypt that I do not remember now. I really wish I could remember what he explained while we were there because I do know it was highly significant and had to do with humanity's future.

When we finished in Egypt, we went to the southwest United States but flew there slowly so I could see sights along the way. I wanted to see this planet with the eyes I had then. I saw the countries of the Far East and the Pacific Ocean. Night was falling in the southwest US and I could see what the being told me was energy emanating from almost everything I could see, especially the plant and animal life. The energy was strongest in the areas of the land and sea that had the least amount of humans.

The energy was the lowest in areas where there were man-made structures, the cities of the world. The energy I saw came from the human beings that lived in the cities. It was explained to me that humans are the basic producers of energy in cities because of their relatively low vibration level the energy is lower in general. I could see the higher sources of energy in the cities though. I was shown people who had higher energy levels and some of them actually talked to the being I was with. I saw dark souls during the time the being and I spent on Gaia. The dark souls were earthbound spirits who refuse to go to the light. They prey on the energies of humans still in human form and try to use those souls to prevent the evolution of spirit. I was told I was protected from these dark ones as long as I chose to focus on the love in me. The dark ones did not even try to affect us, in fact they gave us nasty looks and went away. I was told I would know these dark ones when I see them and I was told to tell them to go to the light. The light is a porthole to the place all souls go if they choose.

I could see energy around the humans too, all different levels and colors. The being explained the human energy to me. He said that the energy coming from humans is what spirits use to evaluate the spiritual condition of particular humans. He said the lighter and more brilliant the color the more advanced the spirit is. He said that seeing the "aura" around a spirit is useful in determining how much a particular spirit needs to work on his development. He said the higher beings know where to go and what to do to help an earthbound soul so they may advance themselves if they so choose. He told me that all souls have this energy, this is why I could see it on every human I saw. He said that I was of the same energy type as he but my vibration is lower when I am in human form and that in time my energy would raise to match his intensity provided I chose to take the initiative to consciously evolve my soul.

He told me that there is much to this planet that spirits can see which humans do not see with their eyes because their vibrations are so low. He showed me life in the trees that I could see as a spirit but could not see in my human form.

He explained that beings of higher vibration do live on Earth but they are not human, they are part of Earth itself. He explained these beings were the caretakers of physical life on the planet. He said that these beings take care of what we call nature. There are beings that take care of the plant life, the mineral life and the waterborne life. These lower echelon beings work together to ensure that all aspects of nature is protected and remains healthy. When the planet was evolving, these ethereal beings were the ones that kept the balance of nature.

He explained to me that the planet that we call Earth really has a proper name. He told me the Earth is really called "Gaia." He said Gaia has its own energy and that Gaia is really a true living being. I asked if this energy could be seen and he said that we have to be away from Gaia to appreciate and see it. He said humans are the ones who can manipulate Gaia's energy through their choices. He said if humans choose to live in harmony with the energy on Gaia, it is good for Gaia. He said if humans abuse Gaia, they hurt Gaia by altering its energy structure. I was given an example of how humans have deforested the planet and reduced the energy available faster than it could be replenished. He said Gaia was very strong but has been weakened considerably since humans have chosen to use the resources in a manner inconsistent with the laws of the universe.

I asked him if we could go into space and see Gaia's energy and he said yes. He said there were no limits on where we could go. I concentrated my thought, trusted, and we then went into what is known as space.

Away from this planet I could see Gaia all at once. It was so beautiful. I could see the aura around Gaia. The aura affected me greatly. I felt a deep love for this beautiful place. I could hear Gaia move and was told the sound was the energy flowing in and out of Gaia. My special being told me that Gaia is the most unique planet because it is designed for humans to live on forever. It was created for a spirit to play, learn, and grow. He said the balance of nature on Gaia allows a spirit to be in human form when a spirit lives in harmony with nature.

Nature exists to compensate for the decreased vibration and was created for spirits to adapt enough to adjust and be in the physical human body while still having access to energy that will help them advance. He explained that humans were designed by God to live eternally on Gaia and are not supposed to "die." He said that "dying" is a human created Earth term that means little in the world of spirit. The reason that humans supposedly die is that they have fallen away from the balance of nature and allow themselves to be affected by what they create that violate the natural laws of the universe. He said that humans have fallen away from living in balance with nature. He said they must relearn about the harmonic balance if they want to survive as a race and live on Gaia forever. He said it was still possible for humans to learn about this harmony and that it is the next overall goal of humans on Gaia. I was told that humans would eventually realize they must restore the harmony but great damage will be inflicted before humans will fully realize what they have been doing to Gaia and work to reverse what they have done.

We traveled past all of the planets in our solar system. Near each planet I could hear the energy just like on Gaia. I saw the auras around each one of them too. I saw spirits on all of them as well. My friend told me that all planets are places for spirits to live, learn and thus evolve. I saw great cities on each and every one of those planets. It was explained that other life in the universe is not readily seen because the beings were all of higher vibration and most spirits in human form have yet to attain the higher vibration required to see them.

The being told me that each planet has a theme for learning and that any of them can be chosen by a soul when we are between physical lives. He said we practice on the other planets to be ready to live on Gaia. He said Gaia is the ultimate experience for a soul. It is ultimate because our souls evolve faster here than anywhere else. It was said that the lessons we need to learn are difficult to learn without having a physical form.

He explained how we pick a physical life on Gaia. He explained to me that I picked the parents I was born to so that I could learn what I needed to learn to grow enough to come back and do spirit work on Gaia after I attain a certain level of growth. He said that I was being told all of these things so that I could help souls come together and return Gaia to harmony.

He explained some things to me about God that I do not remember. They had to do with the universe and the size and structure of it. I do remember he said that God is not to be seen for he is everywhere. He told me that God loves Gaia deeply, much as a man loves his wife.

He talked about Jesus too. He told me Jesus was a master God sent to Earth to teach humans how to act toward each other and find their way back to the path of harmony with each other as well as with Gaia.

I was told that Jesus is the being that is entrusted by God to ensure that souls evolve. He said that Jesus is of the highest in vibration than any other soul. He said that God holds Jesus in the highest of favor because he was the best example of what humans need to do. I then got to see Jesus. I saw his light. Jesus' light was the purest I have ever seen. There was no need for words. There were only love feelings that I cannot even begin to describe.

I was told that loving one another is what souls need to do in order for peace and harmony to be the standard on Gaia.

I was told that there is a hierarchy in the universe that is dedicated to preserving the harmony of the universe. I was told that humans are an integral part of this harmony and that the free will we have is a part of souls that allows humans to provide service to the universe.

After he explained those things to me I was able to see our whole solar system all at once in full color. The planets were all in a line and I could see all of them from Pluto to the sun. I felt very blessed and very important. I was given this great gift and I did not really understand why. There I floated, a being that went out his way to inflict pain on other souls, yet I was never asked about what I had done. In fact I was given the honor of being given answers to questions most people wonder about all of their lives.

I thanked this loving being for explaining and showing me what he did. He told me that there was more for him to show me if I was ready to experience it. I told him I was ready. I did not know why I was chosen but I was not about to question why. It just seemed small to me then.

We started to head back toward Gaia. We went to a place in the shadow of Gaia. It was a great city in the clouds. The city had these beautiful white buildings as far as I could see. I saw spirits living there all of which had vibration but no real physical body. These inhabitants went to and from the buildings - going to work and play too. I saw a place where spirits went to get what I thought was water. There were no vehicles there. Spirits seemed to get around the same way my being and I got around, by flying.

The city had no boundaries that I could see. This was a place full of life of all kinds. There was nature there, many pure plants, trees, and water just like on Gaia but more pure. Nature there was absolutely perfect. It was untainted by human manipulation. This place was just like Gaia only without the problems and negativity. I felt that this was what is called heaven in Earth terms.

I saw spirits going to and from the Gaia and the city. I could tell the development of the spirits going to and from by the energy they emanated. I could see that animals came to and from Earth just like humans do. I could see many spirits leave Gaia with guides and could see spirits returning to Gaia without guides. The being told me that some of the spirits passing were the ones that were doing the work with humans on Gaia. I could make out the type of spirits that were doing the work and the spirits that were coming to the great city to become replenished to eventually go back to Gaia to experience and further evolve. I could feel the emotions of the ones coming back for replenishment. I could feel that some of them were sad, beaten and scared, much like I felt before my being came to me.

My being took me into one of the larger buildings. Inside I saw many spirits working. They were doing things similar to jobs on Earth. When we walked by the spirits, they looked at me. I think they were checking me out because of the being I was with.

We went upstairs and I saw spirits that knew me. They greeted me and asked me how I was doing. They gave me advice of which I do not remember. I thought I was going to be given a job there, but the being knew I thought that and told me that there was something I needed to do first.

I was ecstatic. I was in heaven despite everything I had done during my life on Gaia. I was experiencing what most people only dream about. The love I felt there was the same love I felt when I saw Jesus. I had been searching on Gaia for what was really the same place I was in then. I was searching on Gaia for the feeling I was feeling that very moment. I had found what I spent my whole life searching for. I was truly happy. I was home and I knew it. I was ready to stay and do whatever work I was given to do.

My being took me to another building that was special. It was bigger than the rest and had the greenest foliage I had ever seen growing on it, decorating it like a shrine. We went inside a set of double doors that glowed with life. The inside was decorated with a wood paneling that the being told me was "living" wood from the trees that grew at this wonderful place. He led me to some big double doors and told me to wait on this bench while he went inside.

A bit later he came out of the room. He told me to go into the room and said he would wait for me and to not worry. He cautioned me to ensure that I was truthful with the beings in the room. He said they were not judges, rather they were the ones who evaluated a soul's development based on a soul's history. He told me to remember who I was and to refrain from fear. I knew I had to leave this being sooner or later but I was glad that he would wait for me. I was a little scared to leave him, but I felt that I was protected and knew that I would be protected here.

David's profound life review and lessons learned: I went in and saw a group of several spirits seated at a table. The table was made of the glowing wood and was perfect in every way. The spirits around this table had the highest vibration I had seen so far with the exception of Jesus.

I looked at these beings and recognized them. I do not know where I recognized them from, but they all had a familiarity about them. They just looked at me.

All of a sudden, I saw my parents on Earth before I was born. I saw how they came to be together and watched them have my brother and sister before me. I saw their positive and negative sides and evaluated them according to what I knew I needed to do on Gaia. The beings asked me how and why I picked these particular parents and asked me to tell them. They said I knew how and why I picked them and asked me to tell them why. I do not know where it came from but I did tell them how and why and they agreed with me. I picked them to help them on their path as well as to achieve my learning.

I saw my soul go to my mother and go inside of her. I saw myself being born from an observer standpoint as well as having the actual experience. I proceeded to see my entire life from the observer point of view and from the points of view of those my actions affected. I felt the feelings they felt that directly resulted from things I had done to them. I saw both the positive and the negative things I had done as they had truly happened, nothing was left out or presented inaccurately.

I experienced the harshness of being born again. I experienced leaving heaven and the transit to Gaia. I saw myself as a helpless infant who needed his mother for everything. I experienced my father's love as well as his anger. I experienced my mothers love, her fear and her anger as well. I saw all of the good and bad from my childhood years and re-experienced what I had done then. I felt all of my emotions and the emotions of the souls I had hurt as well as loved. From all of this I learned that it matters deeply what choices I make on Gaia.

I learned just how powerful we humans are and how we can affect each other in positive and negative ways. It was amazing to see how my innocent actions had such a powerful effect on souls that I had no idea I was affecting. The experience was one that I will never forget. I experienced the whole spectrum of feelings of my life in a relatively short period of time as we humans see it. Where I was, time did not really exist.

I could see how I became what I had become on Gaia and why I became that way. Everything I did in my life affected the evolution of the souls around me. I saw the reasons for all of my actions and understood why I did what I had done. There was a place for all of my positive and negative actions. There was no action that was necessarily wrong, but there were actions I took that did not enhance positive growth. I was both a victim and a beneficiary of my actions. This was not a fun experience to go through. I could see how wonderful it could be if one chose to act to affect other souls positively most of the time.

Afterward, the beings in the room asked me questions about what I saw and how I felt about my life up to then. I knew that I had to provide an honest assessment - I could not lie. I hesitated when they asked me whether I affected others more positively than negatively. I thought about lying.

These beings knew what I was thinking and I had to tell them that I felt that I could have done a better job on Gaia. I knew what I had come to Gaia to accomplish and was well on my way to doing that but I knew I was not finished yet. They agreed and told me that I still had many things to do and that I may want to go back and do them. I was told it was understood how difficult it would be for me but it was necessary for the universe for me to finish.

They said that it may be wise to go back and live my life how I had originally planned it.

They said I had set lofty goals for my life on Gaia and the events in my life were achieving the goals I had set.

They said that I originally came to Gaia to learn and share with others using the gifts that I have accumulated over several lifetimes.

They said that I am needed on Gaia to help souls bring themselves and Gaia back to harmony.

They said that I have great potential to affect other souls, to help them grow and that Gaia is the best place to do that. I was told that the events I had experienced thus far were preparing me to make a large contribution to the universe and that my experiences were not to be considered personal attacks in any way. I did not want to accept that, I wanted to stay, I told them that.

I told them I was tired and wanted to stay because life on Gaia is hard and unforgiving. I felt that going back would be dangerous for the universe because I was not advanced enough in my spiritual evolution. They said that was precisely why it would be in my best interest to go back to Gaia.

They said I was more advanced than I give myself credit for.

They said that it was possible for me to stay but I would need to finish my work on Gaia sooner or later. The type of work I was destined for can only be done on Gaia. I could stay if chose to but I would only be prolonging the completion of what I needed to do for this universe.

They explained the fastest way to finish my work would be to go back to Gaia as soon as possible.

I was stunned to say the least. I resorted to bargaining but it was no use. I still did not like living on Gaia and did not really want to go back. These beings understood me but remained firm. I had a decision to make that was really the hardest decision I would ever make.

I did come back to Gaia and am now living the life that I was (later in the experience) told I would live. Believe it or not, I ended up shelving this experience away, classifying it as a really vivid "trip." It was not until I evolved more that I realized the gift I was given.

I share this experience now because I feel it can, if so chosen, spur thought and foster choices that affect the planet in a positive way.

If I learned anything from this experience it was that every choice I make is duly recorded, noted and will return later, when I leave here again.

My goal is to save people the pain that I felt in my review and hasten the evolution of humans on Gaia, helping Gaia as well as the universe.

Again, I wish you all of the love I feel in my heart and I give this love to you.

David's insights from his NDE: I'm one who had a near-death experience and was given a choice to return to this planet in a physical sense again. I chose to return out of love for this planet, a love so great that I would give up the slot I have "back home." I did this also in order to help heal the place through the sharing of what I was shown of the in-between and through the choices I make.

Without the free will to return I wouldn't be here in the physical doing what I am doing. The physical pain, war, poverty, pestilence, horror, rape, murder, abandonment etc. that is here on this planet is the result of humans coming here and making their free choices in order to learn and evolve. Unfortunately learning does tend to create a mess at times and the physical pain and negative vibration is a part of that mess. It makes sense to me that the same free choice concept is instrumental in cleaning up and tweaking things for the better.

In my near-death experience I was also shown that there are many souls in "heaven" who are more than willing to come to this place regardless of the state it is in. I was shown that if I didn't choose to return I would be in the schools that exist in heaven, working toward the growth I need to accomplish regardless of the form I am in. That was an attractive choice to be sure except that I had a problem with how long it would take me to grow enough to do what my soul wishes to do. I have a burning desire to experience other places in other universes and to do that I need to grow more and hone my energy. The prerequisite for that is ensuring that my soul has the IQ for it. I need to learn more.

It's my understanding that a soul can choose to remain in heaven and operate on the level he/she is on to infinity, but I seek more because I know without doubt that there is more. At any rate, the idea remains that for this place to start feeling and looking like heaven is to create the love felt there,

here. I would like to feel that on this planet and I know it can be done. If I need to, I will come back here all over again to make it happen.

The following NDE testimony comes from a Non-Gay NDEr: I was a single mom, working 12-hour days to keep a roof over our heads. My ex had moved on and married. I started a hair salon with an old friend, who turned out to be no friend at all. To call her ruthless would be an understatement. I left the business with nothing. My ex's life was going well, and karma wasn't holding up its end of the bargain. I was bitter, and who did I blame? God, of course. I was working three jobs. One of which had not paid me in eight weeks. Two jobs were in Brooklyn and one was in Staten Island. I was working 50 - 70-hour weeks and barely surviving. I had recently broken up with someone I loved deeply, lost a salon, which was my baby and the fulfillment of every dream I had ever had. I was in pain from a recent car accident. I had gained weight from stress eating. I was at my all time low. I felt despair. I walked into my bedroom and I looked up at the ceiling. I was tired, drained. I had heard that things were looking up for people who had hurt me in my life, who I had considered to be not good people. I didn't understand at all how life worked.

I walked into my bedroom and I looked up at the ceiling and I said, "I don't know who you are God, or how you operate or what matters to you. My ex gets to prosper, with no second thought for his kids, with no financial assistance to his children. My ex-business partner gets to benefit from things I created. I don't know what's important to you or what matters? But I don't want a God like that in my life."

I meant it and He knew it. I was determined that I would live as a shell of myself, empty and vacant, just going through the motions. I would stay alive just to raise my children. But I wouldn't feel anything, no hopes no dreams. I was done.

I went to sleep that night drained and defeated. The next morning I woke up to go to one of my three jobs - the one that hadn't paid me in 8 weeks. I had decided that I would consider it a volunteer job, since I wasn't getting paid. I had become attached to the patients in the nursing home and

I wanted to be there for them. I clicked on the television and went to make breakfast. Immediately I heard in a loud, clear voice, "WE ARE BODY, SOUL AND SPIRIT AND MOST PEOPLE HAVE NO POWER IN THEIR LIFE BECAUSE THEY DON'T GO DEEP ENOUGH TO TOUCH SPIRIT, WHERE ALL THE POWER IS."

I wondered if that was my problem. I wondered if he was talking to me. I had just resolved the night before to stop trying and now what? Now was God talking to me through the television? I had an overwhelming feeling that those words were meant for me. It permeated my soul the whole day and drove me crazy. All I wanted to do was what he said, go deeper and touch Spirit - so I could have the power that he was talking about. I had no idea what that meant or what it would come to mean in my life.

I went through the motions of work for the day wanting to stop at different times and try to "go deeper" but I couldn't because I was surrounded by people. I got home and finished my chores and got ready for bed. It was ten o'clock at night. I remember thinking I had waited all day to do this and now I was finally alone. The anticipation was almost too much.

I went into the place in my mind where one would go to pray. I tried to pray deeper. Next I know I was out of my body and rising up.

As I was trying to pray deeper, instantly I was out of my body. I felt myself rising higher and higher to another dimension. I remember thinking, Oh it's up? This is where everything is, up? Heaven, God, dead people this is where they are in the sky?" And as I thought that, I crossed another dimension and I was instantly in outer space. I was somewhere above the universe in the deep navy blue sky, with millions of stars pulsating with light and energy. It was the most peaceful feeling I had ever felt.

My first thought was, "Oh my God, this is where I'm from. This is my home."

I instantly knew that I was made up of the same particles that the stars and planets and air were made of. I knew this was where I originated from and that I was back home. I heard everything telepathically; no words were heard as sound, they were just there in my mind.

Then I "heard", "He knows every hair on your head, Mindy"

"Every moment matters, and where it matters is in your soul. That's what counts."

I heard everything telepathically; no words were heard as sound, they were just there in my mind instantly, like an instant knowing.

When he said "every moment matters" immediately all the pain of a lifetime drained from the top of my head to tips of my toes. I was being emptied of all the pain and suffering of a lifetime and right behind it I was being filled with what I can only describe as Liquid Love. Words that I had never put together before or even thought of in any way but I knew then that was the only way to describe that feeling. That liquid love completely healed me from head to toe and all fear was gone instantly, along with the confusion and pain of a lifetime.

I now knew I was loved, by God.

He was the one I had questioned and blamed my whole life.

His love was all that mattered. And I felt it. It was now part of me. I felt it in me and continue to.

I was then shown images of the Sun, the Stars and the Moon. The moon started coming closer and closer, bigger and bigger.

I saw the moon's surface. Then I heard "God is the Sun, the Stars and the Moon. Is the moon mad at you Mindy?"

I then understood that God was Omnipotent all powerful and Omnipresent everywhere. He had much bigger things to do than be mad at me.

Then I was shown three Mindys. A flesh Mindy, an outline of a Mindy, like a gingerbread cookie and a wind of Mindy.

I heard, "The wind is your spirit it is one with all. Just like the air from Brooklyn to Staten Island doesn't change, Spirit from one person to another, doesn't change."

For the first time in my life I knew what was meant by we are all one. In the spirit we are all one not in the flesh.

I was then directed to the outline of Mindy it was filled with some type of liquid, up to the ankles.

I heard, "That is your soul. It is empty to your ankles because even though your actions were good you were filled with fear and resentment and God does not attach to fear, resentment or any negativity. Negativity will not fill your soul, but drain your soul."

Then they told me there is another place. I saw three small cardboard boxes, corrugated on the inside. I saw them fall to the wayside. I understood that there is a lower place, another dimension.

The thought came to me "What if I go back and do it again? How will I know what to do?"

Now that I realized I am a part of what's happening in my life, I wanted to make sure I didn't recreate the bad.

Immediately I was told, "You will know by the Word".

I had no use of my ears. All information was placed directly into my mind.

I was directed to a silver beam of light higher up in the sky to my left. It was perfectly radiant light with sparks of life. It had a pulse. It was floating and alive. The beam appeared to have energy. Words started to appear on either side of the beam - hundreds of words. Good words on the right bad words on the left.

I heard, "You will know by the Word. Good words have good energy. Bad words have bad energy. There is no grey area. Your life will go in the direction of your thoughts, and it can't be based on your circumstances. that is the meaning of free will here on earth, that is the only meaning of free will, and it your responsibility to fill your soul."

I then saw my ex-husband and ex business partner in the same context of body, soul and spirit. I was told, "Forgive them for they know not what they do, and what they do is to their soul."

I remember looking around experiencing this overwhelming presence and power of the universe. It went on forever. I was told, 'There is no time and no space."

In fact I knew that it is ever increasing, it goes on forever. I also know that wherever I was, was very dense with souls - very crowded. There was so much more going on, more than I 'saw' or experienced.

I was told "You are in the aethers".

I still get chills when I relive those words. I had never heard that word, aethers, before. When I came back from the other side. I looked it up.

Wikipedia defines it as follows: "According to ancient or medieval science, aether (Greek) also spelled ether, also called quintessence, is the material that fills the region of the universe above the terrestrial sphere..."

So I looked it up in Dictionary.com and one of their definitions is "The upper regions of space; the clear sky; the heavens." I have come to understand that the aethers are the In-Between, the space between Heaven and Earth.

I was in the In-Between.

For a split second I saw an image of a peaceful man in a blue turban and my impression was that there are many religions and one was no better than the other. I saw two profiles of faces. Eye to eye. Face to face. Floating, looking into each other's eyes and at the same time I 'heard' "Tell others."

For a split second I saw an image of a peaceful man in a blue turban and my impression was that there are many religions and one was no better than the other. I saw two profiles of faces. Eye to eye. Face to face. Floating, looking into each other's eyes and at the same time I 'heard' "Tell others."

They wanted me to tell people what happened and what I had learned. I thought that was odd. It seemed like an impossible task. Who would believe it? I was to follow these instructions and try to put them to use in my everyday life. I was then shown an elderly white man -- pale, thin and frail. He was wearing boxer shorts. Floating in a hospital bed in outer space. He had white facial stubble. I was told that when someone suffers at the end of their life there is a reason and a purpose, a sort of burning away of karma. Although that word was never used, there would be a benefit on the other side.

I woke up. It was the next day. I was back. I don't know how long I was there. That drove me crazy for a long time, until I finally gave up trying to figure it out. Was I there ten minutes or ten hours? It didn't matter. I woke up knowing that I was forever changed.

I was not the same person I was when I had gone to bed. I was elated, floating. Everything was different.

At first I felt like I was a newborn baby. I was a stranger in a new world. I was joyful for the first time in my life and now I knew the rules.

The following NDE testimony comes from a Gay NDEr: On June 2nd, 1995 I had what is commonly called, "a near-death/out-of-body experience." This event occurred because of a reaction to medications I was taking while having dental surgery performed. Two weeks prior to going in for the dental surgery, I had injured myself while lifting a big screen TV up a long flight of stairs in the rain. Once at the top, I slipped and lost my footing. While I did manage to catch the TV, I pulled out several major muscles in my lower back. Because the medications I was on were not powerful enough to ease the pain, I remained bedridden for over a week. I was later given an even stronger painkiller so that I might get up and move around. On the day of my dental surgery, now weary of the thought of any additional pain and discomfort, I purposefully took a rather large dose of the pain killer before my dental appointment thinking that would save me from feeling anything. Because I was very nervous that particular day, I had a lapse in my memory, and forgetting that I had already taken some pills ... I took another handful! By the time I got to the dentist's office, I was feeling a bit woozy ... But because I had forgotten I had taken that extra handful of pills, I really didn't think I was in any danger. Actually, I felt pretty good. But then the inevitable happened:

The large dose of pain killers ended up conflicting with the anesthesia given to me in the dentist's office and the result was that my blood pressure fell to low and I was literally knocked unconscious and right out of my body. During a brief amount of time, my spirit traveled through what I know and now call, "the Heavenly Realm." During the experience, all time stopped ... and two minutes of Earth time turned into what seemed to be days, weeks and even months. I saw an uncountable amount of wonderful places that were not of this world and many spiritual truths were Lovingly and generously revealed to me with mind-bending answers. Almost the whole time I was guided mostly by a being that appeared in the form of the most beautiful woman I have ever seen. Following us were three other guides who all appeared as men. All were robed with a beautiful glistening white, diamond-like material. I could also distinguish that they had Light coming from underneath their garments. I knew that this Light was their true bodies. The moment they came into my awareness, I recognized these beings as having been some of my closest friends that have been with me for all time. They were very kind to me and very caring about my feelings. There are no secrets in Heaven, so information that might have been considered embarrassing was treated with tremendous sensitivity. And even in moments where I might have cried knowing that someone knew my deepest darkest secrets, wonderful warm laughter was often exchanged between us instead. No matter any unpleasantness they may have known about me, I knew that I was eternally and unconditionally Loved! For many years, after my experience, I have continued to stay in contact with these dear ones through dreams and meditations. During my experience it was revealed to me that they had made many appearances to me during my life, particularly during difficult times in my childhood and adolescence, only I was not consciously aware of them or their presence at the time.

WHEN YOU PASSED OVER, DID YOU SEE GOD IMMEDIATELY?

At first, I did not see God immediately. However, I did FEEL the presence of God everywhere! When I found myself in the Realm, initially I spoke with my very Loving guides, absorbed amazing information and took in the bigness of everything that was shown to me in God's Heaven. Then, toward the end of my experience, I stood in the wonderful presence of a great Being of brightness and knew with my whole heart that I was in the midst of my Creator, who is a being of unconditional Love and infinite Light. Many of you will not yet remember, but you too have stood in the very presence of God! I saw that before each of us are sent forth into our various missions, we are brought into a vast Cathedral of Light known as, "the Throne Room of God." In this room resides the very essence of all Creation, the Being those of us who are Jewish or Christian know and call Father God. This Being is the author of all that exists and he is tremendously pleased with all that has come forth from his Light. Because our Souls are covered by what is known as a "veil of forgetfulness," we are made to seek God out in ways that hopefully has us seeking him in each other. Each of us carries the Light of the Creator within us and it is through this experience we call "life in a flesh" that helps us to better understand the Creator and develop the inner Light he placed within us by practicing Love. A time will come soon enough where we will be back in the Loving arms of God and it will be a very Joyous time for us all. But first we must work at accomplishing the thing he sent us here to learn ... LOVE!

WHEN YOU GOT TO HEAVEN, WHAT WAS THE FIRST THING YOU SAW?

When I arrived in Heaven (in my experience) I found myself in a huge room where the walls and ceilings were made of pure crystal and they had Light coming from the inside of them. The effect was amazing. Then as I looked up, I saw four translucent screens appear (and form a kind of gigantic box around me). It was through this method that I was shown my life review. (Or rather I should say my LIVES IN REVIEW!) Without ever having to turn my head, I saw my past, my present, my future and there was even a screen that displayed a tremendous amount of scientific data, numbers and universal codes. I saw the beginning of my known existence as a Soul and saw that I had existed Spiritually long before this incarnation -- where I am now a male human known as Christian Andréason! In Heaven, I undeniably saw that I had lived an innumerable amount of lives. Yet, what I saw went way beyond our comprehension of what we think reincarnation is. So, I am not exactly speaking of being born again and again on this planet alone. I saw that it is a big Universe out there and God has it all organized perfectly. Each of us is sent where we can obtain the best growth according to our Divine purpose.

Before the review ended, I was shown something that blows my mind every time I think about it. I observed myself go before what I understood to be as the Throne of Heaven. This is a great domed hall in the center of a golden city and is where the highest presence of God exists. What I saw was nothing short of spectacular!

IN SHORT, WHAT DID YOU SEE?

As I entered the room, I was washed with a brilliant white, golden and rose colored Light which filled me with indescribable happiness. I knew this Light had created me, as it had everything else. The Light was God ...

both Father and Mother Creator mixed together in a colorful body of Light I have since learned to call, Christ.

As I looked up, the Light went on and on without end. I was lifted high up into the Great Light, and as this happened, I felt fully embraced by my Creator. I knew without a doubt that this omnipresent being found great delight in me and I clearly heard thoughts that I was considered a perfect being of the Creator's Creation.

WHAT WERE YOU TOLD?

I was told many things. But one thing has always stuck out in my mind: each of us have pre-planned moments where what I call, "clue events" will occur. These moments always trigger a memory that Heaven planted deep in the subconscious mind before we came here ... and once set off, the memory makes its way up to the more conscious part of our brain and enters our main stream of thought. This event then evokes a future thought or feeling in us, which sooner or later produces an action that gets us walking in the direction toward our destiny. If you understand the concept of "déjà vu" you know what I am talking about. In Heaven, I saw over and over again, things that we see almost on a daily basis, which might even seem mundane ... could actually be clues for us to pick up on to get us going in the right direction! I understood that before we came to Earth, many of these clues were shown and explained to us and in our spirit we hold a deep knowing of what any particular clue really means for us. I saw that the conscious mind does not need to recognize a clue, (although Spiritually sensitive people will eventually begin to discern them), it is the eternal "subconscious" part of the mind that does all the spiritual work for us. A clue can come in the form of us looking at a clock at just the right moment and seeing a set of numbers that mean something to us ... it can be hearing someone say a familiar phrase or "trigger word" at a very interesting period of your life ... or it can be something as simple as seeing a single item sitting somewhere odd that intrigues you to wonder ... "Why is that thing there?"

I was then shown the time we call the beginning of Creation. There was a huge explosion, coming from a singing, pulsing, Joy-filled ball of bright Golden Light. I knew that I had been a part of this great Light, as have the rest of us. From this Light exploding, I found myself happily and quite excitedly hurling through space and time. I arrived safely in a perfect place of peace and amazing splendor. I knew immediately that this place was geared toward the expansion and education of every Soul that came there. I call this place, "the Realm." In this place, we are assisted by many wise beings and helped to complete many years of training and Soulish expansion.

WHERE IS THE HEAVENLY REALM?

In all honesty, the Realm is all around us, and not just above ... but directly in front of us. It is hard to see, but it is there. Heaven exists in another dimension that can only be entered by the way of Spirit. There are many different Heavens and Realms of Heaven. They are stacked one atop the other like pancakes and scattered all throughout God's super Universe. Each sits at a level that can accommodate those who walk within it. At the highest level is the Master Creator, God, and at the lower levels are the various forms and presence(s) of God. Everything is regulated by vibration, current and frequency ... the higher our spirit's level of vibration and frequency, the higher our Spirits are able to go throughout the Divine Realm. God, the Creator, vibrates at an absolute level that is so fast that he is perfectly still. His frequency is incomprehensible and is ever-expanding upward in pitch.

WHAT DOES HEAVEN LOOK LIKE?

Glorious. There are many levels and dimensions in the Realm. There are great cities very similar to the ones we live in now, only these places have great harmony and balance to them. I saw whole cities made of gold and precious stones. One city that always stays in the back of my mind is a great metropolis made entirely out of what looked to be sapphires. It glows with the most luminous blue and white Light. It reminds me of a white Christmas tree with beautiful blue glass balls. I had a knowing that this place was where Loving Christ-like communicators choose to gather and exchange thoughts. There is a tremendous amount of Love and Grace in Heaven. No matter where you go, the feeling of Love and Joy is everywhere. There is no other place you would rather be.

IS THERE A SPECIAL PLACE WHERE WE STAY IN HEAVEN?

The point to incarnating in a physical body is so that once we are done, we can then explore the many worlds and places of wonder within the Realm. However, each of us is allowed a sacred space there, (where we can make a home for our Soul), if we desire to. (I will explain more about this below.)

HOW DOES HEAVEN CHANGE IN APPEARANCE?

The higher up you go in Heaven, the more it becomes impossible to give a human description. I try to explain it by saying there are flashes of Light and brilliant colors of every spectrum everywhere. In fact the colors that are in Heaven are more brilliant than the ones we have here on Earth. There are healing tones that play incredible music, which all together form one single sacred song. There is such tremendous LOVE, PEACE and JOY there that you can think of no other place you would rather be. There is no way to really describe the high Heavens. It has to be experienced by the individual. And all individuals will have this experience when they are ready and it is time for them.

SO EARTH IS NOT OUR HOME?

Earth is home for the physical human body, which is temporary ... even the Earth is temporary. But Heaven is made of pure, radiant Light that lasts forever and ever. Heaven could certainly be said to be our real home, however; as we Spiritually mature we will continuously move up and up until we are once again reunited with the Creator of all Creation.

WHO GOES TO HEAVEN?

In the end ... believe it or not (sigh of relief), everyone gets to come home! Heaven is a place of ultimate LOVE. When we have learned how to become individuals that base our entire existence and consciousness around manifesting LOVE, we then become capable of entering the domain of the higher Realms of Heaven. If we do not practice Love, we can only go so far and we will be made to incarnate somewhere out there in God's super Universe again and again (unlimited times) until we learn.

WHAT GOES ON IN THE "DIVINE REALM?"

Lots of things! Individuals are laughing, relaxing and enjoying one another's company. Some are off working together in pairs (or larger), so that they might bring a new concept or idea, or accomplish a Divinely intended goal for the planet. Some are off to themselves reflecting in far away, peaceful places and learning how to work with and trust the power they hold within them. Others form close-knit groups and enjoy learning together as they are taught by various Loving, advanced teachers and guides of Spirit. The Realm is a real happening place I can tell you that! I always laugh when I think of society's image of Heaven as little cherubs sitting around playing harps on clouds. Ahhhh ... it's a whole lot more intense than that!

WHO CAN SEE HEAVEN OR THE DIVINE REALM?

Anyone can see it.

EVEN IN THE BODY?

Yep. Even in the body. You will be amazed to find out that some of the things you "thought you saw" (but thought your mind was playing tricks on you) were actually things Heaven was helping you see on Earth. Again, the higher up you go in your capacity to hold Love and Light in your Soul, the greater the chance your spirit will reside long enough in your body to help your consciousness become open enough to help you see and understand the Realm.

HOW CAN I LEARN HOW TO SEE IT?

Every time you choose to participate in a LOVING THOUGHT, you are manifesting the feeling of HEAVEN ON EARTH. The reason most are so unsure about the place from which we all came is because we have not yet learned to LOVE ourselves or one another enough. Once we learn how to LOVE enough and keep this LOVE perpetual, we will build up a tremendous inner Light and this Light will be used to help us see glimpses into Heaven. Not only will you be able to see or sense spiritual things, you will also understand how to work through issues that trouble you in your life.

For many, seeing or sensing Spiritually can happen quite suddenly. Close your eyes and take a deep breath. ALLOW the peace, presence and Joy of Almighty God to wash over you like a warm, gentle, flowing stream of water. Concentrate on this feeling for as long as you are able. Just imagine to your best ability what the word "JOY" might mean to you. If you feel doubt or have "jumbled" emotions about this word, it could mean that you are holding guilt, shame or unforgiveness in your Soul. These things have no place in the Realm of God! Let them go now. Think only what it means to LOVE and be LOVED. Be patient.

WHAT WILL I SEE WHEN I SEEK TO SEE HEAVEN?

Some report to having seen their silver cord, some see white flashes of Light, some see tunnels of dark blue or violet with a lovely blue pastel color toward the end. Some of you may even see moving figures, buildings, colorful flower gardens or even great celestial cities. Others report having amazing consciousness expanding thoughts come to them which help them to understand their lives, the world and the ultimate plan of God better.

DO WE HAVE A HOME IN HEAVEN?

As a matter of fact, (as I said before) I saw that we do (should we want one) and this home can be as wonderful as we wish it to be! It can be a quaint cottage or it can even be a huge mansion. Real estate is not an issue in Heaven! If you can think it, it can be done. What many of us fail to realize is that each of us DOES have the ability to manifest any visualization into material form. In Heaven, because all things are made from the essence of pure LIGHT, this process is done much easier. In Heaven, we have the ability to sculpt density into the Light (using concentration) and this is how we create form throughout the Realm. We do this by lightly focusing (or pressing) with our intention. You would be amazed at how much you could accomplish here on Earth once you master the art of concentration.

WHAT DID YOUR HOUSE LOOK LIKE IN HEAVEN?

I saw that I had a house made entirely of rubies. These precious stones were affixed to the walls in the hundreds of thousands to millions. I saw that I have a very pleasant home in the Realm. It actually has a flowing stream that moves through the house and into a lovely, lush, floral garden in the back. I saw that the furniture was very similar to what we have here on Earth, only more round and simplistic and with much more cushion. Surprisingly, texture is something that can very much be felt in Heaven. In fact, all of our five senses are very much the same as on Earth, only in

Heaven, they are far more developed. We have the ability to smell, see, hear, touch and get ready .... YES!!! EVEN TASTE!!!! Oh, yes children! THERE IS A GOD!

DID GOD SHARE WITH YOU WHAT YOUR PURPOSE WAS IN THIS LIFE?

Yes. I remember God conveying to me that I would know times of great jubilation and that there would also be times that I would know sorrow as I pursued my ordained purpose. But I was told that I would be blessed for every time I succeeded in the name of Love. I was told that every experience was extremely necessary according to a greater plan that would unfold plans and plans never-ending. I was told not to ever worry about my competency, capacity or ability, for it was promised to me that the Light would never leave me to endure anything I was not created to handle. I was told that there would be times I would doubt myself and my mission, but in the end, I would learn great wisdom and eventually see myself as victorious.

I was shown an innumerable amount of scenes, all containing possible realities I would eventually experience. I was shown many Universes and worlds that had organizational life on them. I saw that everyone in every Universe is simultaneously working together to fulfill God's great Divine plan. I understood that God sees and knows absolutely everything that happens everywhere. I saw that while God does a great deal of planning, our Creator never interferes with our volition, nor does he ever seek to alter the way we feel about things. God knows he need not interfere because he knows that the law of cause and effect is always perfect. This method will always bring justice and teaching wherever it is needed most.

I was amazed to see how each of us is connected eternally, that we have always existed, and that we will never die.

I saw that we were indeed made in the image of God, which is an essence taken from the Creator's own LIGHT. It is because of this Light that we can never die. Every single child of God carries this Light within their Soul, and we call this Light, Spirit. As we learn how to LOVE, we build the Light of Spirit within. A day will come (in a time not so far away) when all of our Light(s) will have become so large that we will merge and go back to the Creator and be as ONE -- just as we were in the beginning. Once we are ONE again, there will be a great celebration. And after a certain amount of time has passed, yet again, there will be another great explosion, only this time it will be much bigger and the process of Creation will be far more advanced.

I felt tremendous Joy and honor in having been shown these things and with great confidence, I promised my God that I would do my very best. God told me my best would certainly be enough!

WHY IS IT SO IMPORTANT TO UNDERSTAND LOVE AND USE IT IN EVERYDAY LIFE?

The reason why we must learn Love on Earth can be given a scientific explanation. God is Love and absolute vibration. The act of Christ-like Love elevates inner vibration. As we learn how to Love and practice Christ-like Love with one another, the inner vibration within the Soul creates supernatural inner Light. This Light helps us to enter various dimensions that lead the way to the Heavens once we are in spirit form. Contrary to what many of us were taught in our various religions, "Heaven" is not a reward for good behavior, it is a "higher plane of existence" that awaits those who ready themselves to enter. The only way to enter through the door ... is to hold the key of Love.

HOW CAN I LEARN MORE ABOUT THE WAYS OF LOVE?

Jesus Christ came to the planet to be a way-shower for all people and all religions. He lived his life with great passion and dedication to this word LOVE, so that each of us might have a role model to compare ourselves to. This is why he said, "I AM the way, I AM the truth, and I AM the life. No man can come to God but through me. If you replace I AM and ME with LOVE IS ... you get ...

LOVE is the WAY

LOVE is the TRUTH

LOVE is the LIFE.

No one comes unto GOD unless they know how to LOVE

Christ had become LOVE WALKING AND TALKING ON THE PLANET. One cannot understand God until one understands and

WALKS AND TALKS in the ways of LOVE. If you walk in Love, you will always understand God.

HOW DOES ONE KNOW WHETHER OR NOT HE OR SHE IS WALKING IN THE WAYS OF LOVE?

1. They are not easily offended (if at all) and they are always willing to forgive trespass! (This is a biggie!)
2. They are generous people who give wholeheartedly.
3. They have a positive non-oppressive relationship with God that is continually growing.
4. They do all they can to be of service to others and bring beauty to the planet.

DID YOU SEE ANGELS?

Yes, Angels were everywhere, however; though Angels are very important to my mission, they were not always the focal point of my experience. Of course, the ones with wings were always somewhere in the background, watching and Lovingly serving in any way they possibly could. One of my greatest memories was when I found myself standing in the highest Heaven, in the area I know to be the Throne Room. As I looked up, I saw the most awesome celestial event of dark purple and blue. I also saw thousands of Angels with many eyes and wings shining through and looking down on me. These beings were interconnected and formed a gigantic circle and I knew that they were of great importance to God. I saw these beings as the keepers and guardians of all knowledge. These beings were gigantic and I had a knowing that they could instantly evaporate anything (that has been formed from fear and darkness) with a single thought. But as they looked upon me, I felt such tenderness, compassion, safety and LOVE. Their greatest concern was always for my happiness and that I be pleased with what I was being told and shown.

HOW MANY ANGELS DO EACH OF US HAVE?

As many as we need. Some need one, but I understand that most have two or even three. These Angels mostly come in the form of guides.

However, winged guardian Angels are never far away and always have a watchful eye on us to make sure nothing prevents us from accomplishing our Divine purpose.

WHO ARE OUR GUIDES AND WHAT ARE THEIR ROLES IN OUR LIVES?

Our guides are what I call our wingless Angels. They are our most cherished friends and supporters in Heaven. They never leave our side ... Never for a single second. In fact, what many do not know is that somewhere right here on Earth, in our families or somewhere in a line of dear personal friends, there is always one who acts as a Heavenly go between for us and the Realm. Hence the verse, "Angels walk among you unaware!"

WHAT WERE YOU SHOWN ABOUT CHRIST, AS BEING THE SON OF GOD?

I think it is very important to start off by saying that I fully saw and understood that we are ALL the children of God. Each and every one of us plays a vital role on this planet. No one is seen as insignificant or is unloved. I understood that to be called a son or daughter of God, means that you have matured fully in all the ways of LOVE. Jesus IS the great leader for all the Sons and Daughters of God, especially those who follow the Christian faith. It was made very clear to me that Jesus does not want anyone bowing down to him and being subservient. In fact, what Christ truly wants us to feel is that we are worthy to walk right beside him. Only through our agreement to walk beside Christ can there be any real progress made in our lives and in the world.

WHY WOULD YOU RECOMMEND THAT SOMEONE GET TO KNOW CHRIST?

For many years, I had no clue who this man Jesus Christ was. Oh, I was raised up to be a Christian alright ... but I never really understood who Christ really was until after my experience. I found too many in Christianity come off as haughty and oppressive ... and because of this ... I wanted to distance myself as far away from the faith as I could! But in the process, I also distanced myself from Jesus, The teacher of Love and that was unfortunate! It was not Jesus' fault that so many who 'said' they

subscribed to the Lord of Love's ways ... came off acting like they had a
board up their backside! Perhaps if I had had better examples of Christ-
Love as a child, I would have understood the Lord when I was first taught
to believe in him, but that was not in the cards for me.

So now, I never EVER judge anyone if they are unsure about what they
feel when it comes to God, Christ or the Bible. I have found ... you cannot
rely on humankind or a single book to reveal God to you ... you have to
seek these things out with all your whole heart and let the Holy Spirit be
your guide. In time because of suffering ... I wanted to see the truth ... and
the Holy Spirit showed me: Christ is the light of God that we each hold
within us and will awaken to when we choose to embody a Loving lifestyle.
The more we do such a thing (and put faith based Love into practice) ...
the better our lives will become and the more we reveal this inner Light
to ourselves and others.

A great number of people on the planet may think they know Christ,
but it is clear that they do not. They have not yet passed the Love test. You
can always tell who has Christ and who does not ... simply by watching
how a person consistently treats people. Sure, some people might have a
bad day or two and totally blow their cool, but I am talking about a person
who in their heart has a sense of urgency to want to Love on and Joyously
Serve others, and not just the ones who look or behave attractively ... but
all people. A person filled with the Christ Light will always see that every
Soul on this planet is a precious child of our Creator and will always
do hers or his best to Love on them with all their might! YOU WILL
ALWAYS HEAR ME SAY THIS OVER AND OVER ... LOVE IS THE
ONLY WAY TO GO! I cannot say it enough, because this is the path to
understanding God and Christ in Heaven. The more you use it and put it
into practice ... the more you will evoke the Spirit of the living God in you
and see this for yourself. I would Love it if you understood God and Christ
better ... so that you would once and for all see that Love is an awesome
energy ... it's a tool that makes you more powerful than you could ever
imagine! Another vital thing to understand about Love ... is that it also
shows you that you and all others are worthy to call out to God or Christ

and receive help at any time. Not only will the Light of God come, but Angels will come running too. We may not see the manifestation of this all at once, but God is always there ... especially when we call!

Another reason I really want some of you to consider Christ, is if by some chance you feel like you get lost ... especially at the time of your physical death. You can call on Christ and he will come for you!

WHAT ABOUT THE FACT THAT CHRISTIAN RELIGION SAYS WE ARE TO WORSHIP GOD AND/OR CHRIST?

Too many do not understand the difference between "worship" and spending time in the presence of God Almighty ... If you want to bask in absolute appreciation for our Creator's Love and Goodness, then that is wonderful! Doing this will only empower you to see that you are a very precious child in God's Creation. The Joy of the Lord is our Strength! I always encourage those I work with Spiritually (all of my one-on-ones) to seek out and spend time every day in the presence of God. Nothing can be better! But some believe that unless they are face down on the floor or performing some repellant activity or major form of sacrifice, that they are not properly worshiping or "earning" God's Love. I saw very clearly in Heaven that God expects nothing of the sort from us ...and that we need not seek to earn anything from God, because everything has already been given! HOWEVER ... WE ARE HERE TO HAVE ABSOLUTE RESPECT FOR THE GLORY OF GOD and OPEN OURSELVES TO RECEIVE GOD'S LOVE, SO THAT WE MIGHT BE ABLE TO GIVE LOVE TO OTHERS! In fact, if you really want to know what true worship looks like, it is how you treat others, when you are kind and gracious with them.

Modern day religion has no real concept of just how humble God and Christ are. If they did, they would never utter one single unloving word to any child of God! As for me, I have personally chosen to see Jesus, the Christ, as the true example of what a Holy Child of God should be like. I also personally believe that he is perhaps the greatest man that has yet to walk the planet. I know in my heart of hearts that each and every one of us aspires to become the same. After my experience, I found the scripture in the Bible where Christ said, "Great things I have done, but greater you will do!" He said this because he wants us to join him in relationship to God. I have nothing but total respect and LOVE for this man, Jesus. While I never saw his human "face" during my experience -- later on it came to my realization that I had seen Christ, only, I experienced him in a way that I wasn't looking for.

HOW CAN A PERSON BECOME LOST AFTER DEATH? DON'T WE JUST PASS ON?

While God always Loves us and never turns away from us, when the time comes for us to crossover ... some may decide not to go into the Light and remain earthbound for a time. This is a very difficult kind of experience and there are a great number of Souls who exist in this station right now. In fact, much of my one-on-one practice is helping those who have the energy of earthbound Spirits hitchhiking in their spiritual atmosphere. When I observe that an angry energy is attached to someone, I see that these beings are lost ...and most have not yet found God or Love during their physical lives ... so now they feel confused, bewildered, caught or trapped. And (in a moment of struggle) they feel as if they have no other choice but to siphon off the Light(s) of others ... who are still alive and in a physical body.

WHY DOES GOD ALLOW A SOUL ENERGY TO SIT ON THE ENERGY OF SOMEONE ELSE?

In my NDE I saw that God had built the Soul to be a kind of net that retrieves or catches energy within it. Doing so not only causes the netting Soul to grow spiritual muscle (by being consistently weighted down by the energy in his or her net) ... but it also gives transport to a lost being ... also giving the lost one an opportunity to observe us during moments where we practice Love and/or remember our inner Divinity. When a Soul is lost in the nether regions (between this dimension and the Realm) or in what the Bible calls, "the death shadowed valley," it is because they do not remember who they are in Christ ... and have forgotten Love.

Therefore, God gives lost Souls an opportunity to grow by allowing them to closely monitor us.

WHAT HAPPENS TO A PERSON WHOSE LIGHT IS BEING SIPHONED?

The event of being "siphoned" into can cause some very difficult issues to happen for an individual being tapped into ... especially if the person has attracted to them too many unloving energies. Remember: we attract to us energetically what we are (as an energy) ourselves. Over time ... if our behaviors are risky and unloving ... this kind of thing can cause us to feel very "weighted down!" Some people start to have overt feelings that appear very foreign to their Soul or addictive behaviors (minor and serious) may begin to crop up and gradually take over. They may have energy problems or feel constantly depressed, angry, ill, jealous, resentful, lazy or fatigued. People all the time will tell me, "I keep finding myself doing or saying or feeling things I don't want to do, say or feel!" Paul in the Bible used to say this very thing himself ... and then openly speak about something he called his, "thorn in the flesh" which God would never remove from him. We all have these "thorns" and it is in God's plan that we learn how to deal with them, by learning how to properly deal with the emotions we feel within ourselves. This is one of the many methods God will use to drive a Soul into development.

When people come to me about issues that "seemed to suddenly come up during a certain difficult period in their lives ... which do not easily go away" ... this can be an indication that a person is in a process of what I call, "holding" too much spiritual energy on their Light-body that does not really belong to them. And sure enough, when I clairvoyantly look at a person who has come to see me, I will clearly see the presence of many energies who have all not yet crossed over. All of them will be firmly latched to the person, for the same purpose or reason as one would be holding onto a life raft in the middle of the ocean. Actually, (believe it or not) this kind of thing is quite normal, as each of us attracts energies of like kind toward us at every hour of every day from other dimensions. However, I find with energies who are causing problems, we can draw the presences of these energies too near to our core Self and this can greatly affect how we think and see ourselves. Think of having multiple personality disorder and you will somewhat grasp what I am saying. I have noticed when it comes to these energetic beings, many of them do not feel comfortable with God's Love or Christ ... and they are unsure as to whether or not they have the right to call out and claim their Divine birthright of receiving salvation. When I see this ... I know that there is a strong likelihood that the person in front of me ... "holding" ... might have similar issues as well, as I always keep in mind the laws of attraction draw to us what we are. So in my one-on-ones, I do what I call "Soul retrieval/Love revival work" and I work with an individual to get them to create as much Christ centered Love in their lives as possible, so they can eventually cause an explosion of inner Light that not only puts proper distance between them and the visitor(s), but a proper barrier for what we would think of as evil as well.

Long story now made short ... I do not recommend that you follow the path of some of these Souls who become earthbound. When your time comes ... and the Light, the tunnel, Christ or your departed Loved ones come for you to take you home ... go with them and go to Heaven! That is where you really belong! Just know that when you Love God or Christ ... you will just naturally sense of feel where you need to go in Heaven and arrive in that place automatically.

WHAT IS GOD MADE OF?

God is an essence of absolute Love, Light and beautiful sound. What I understood (in Christian practice) to be the WORD of God, is actually the SOUND or MUSIC of God.

God is a great LIGHT-filled Being who sings all tones simultaneously and uses this method to bring all things into existence ... He causes each Creation to resonate with one another in perfect harmony, once that Creation has aligned itself with the ways of Love. God uses his SOUND to create all things and give them life. He then extends his Light and helps that Creation to take form. All of us hold Light and Tones within ... We are here to learn how to better use them by living life in a difficult environment for the spirit and Soul ... the physical body.

HOW LONG IS THE LIGHT OF GOD WITH US? IS THERE ANYTHING WE CAN DO TO MAKE IT GO AWAY?

Once God extends his Light, that Light will remain with that Creation for all eternity. There is nothing that can remove it. Each and every one of us is surrounded by a great beacon of Light. This is our eternal cord that connects us to our Creator. When most speak of seeing a tunnel (in NDE experiences) what they are referring to is the cord that ever connects us to God and the Light of Heaven shining through it from up above.

HOW IS IT THAT YOU WERE SHOWN THESE THINGS?

I am not quite sure of what ALL the reasons might be; I do know I was destined to be some kind of teacher on this planet and I think that is obvious ... but one thing is sure ... I am so glad my NDE happened cause God knows I really, really needed it! All I can say is ... I have been very blessed and very assisted to get to this level of understanding. I have worked very hard to be a Loving person all my life and I have endured my fair share of heartache. Much of my childhood was filled with abuse, neglect and harsh experiences and at times my adulthood has been far from being a piece of cake too. But I do not lament over this, because I know that these difficulties caused me to grow in spiritual strength. Yet, there is another thing I think about that might have caused the NDE ... perhaps I got too lost inside my shattered perceptions (during moments of pain) and started going in the opposite direction of what God's true plan for my life was?

One thing I know about God, is he always comes to get us if we get too lost in our lives. My experience put me back on the path and I work daily to stay on it, but even still, I still fall off from time to time. Now having said all this, it is important to know that every single person can know and see all I have. They just have to get themselves to a place of Love so they can.

SO YOU ARE SAYING THAT I CAN I HEAR FROM GOD? IF SO, HOW?

Yes! I am saying that ANYONE can hear from God! One does not need to be Moses or Jesus or Buddha to hear from their Creator. To hear from God, all one has to do is THINK as the CREATOR thinks. Well, I happen to know that God thinks only ONE central thought, so this should be easy for you! GOD THINKS ABOUT NOTHING BUT LOVE -- ALL THE TIME!

If you are living your life according to the ways of LOVE. (Which are the constructive ways that you know deep down in your spirit that are right for you), then you can confidently know that you have the ability to hear from God. If you are actively seeking to spend time in the presence of God ... then you can bet Spirit is going to provide opportunities for you to do that! You will always know when the presence of God is with you ... you will feel like a grateful and excited little child again.

Actually all of us hear from God every day, only we are not aware of it. Because we can get so caught up with the illusions and ego distractions of this world, we can lose focus easily. It is like being immersed in an action-packed movie or book while someone is speaking, only you find yourself looking up and saying, "huh?" once you realize they have been speaking to you for some time.

HOW DO I KNOW IF I AM HEARING FROM GOD?

Anything that is not of LOVE is not of God! PERIOD! If thoughts of judgment, condemnation, bitterness, unforgiveness, ego centered anger or hate based retaliation come into your mind and dominate it, please know, this is not God. This is your ego speaking, which is ruled by fear. God fears nothing, therefore; God can speak no thing that is reminiscent of fear. God only speaks using a language of Love.

WHAT ABOUT SEXUALLY DIVERSE PEOPLE?

If this world was to ever find out just a small amount of what sexually diverse (gay) people are here to do on this planet, there would never be one single wisecrack or hurtful remark made ever again. Instead there would be great respect! People who speak disrespectful things about people of this orientation ... enact judgment, and do so from a place of unenlightenment, insecurity, ego and socially induced prejudice. Some may use mistranslated scriptures taught to them, not by the Holy Spirit ... but by fear-filled human beings. Many will choose to sustain a Divinely unsupported satanic hate-based rage against these children of God, rather than using Love to bring understanding and healing between both peoples. Christ said, THE GREATEST COMMANDMENT IS THAT WE ARE TO LOVE ONE ANOTHER! When people sling condemnation, judgment and bitterness at others, they are not practicing the great commandment. They are allowing their Souls to fall into darkness.

WHAT WERE YOU TOLD OR SHOWN ABOUT THIS ISSUE?

When I got to Heaven, one of the first things I asked was about the very issue of bisexuality, as it had caused me a great deal of concern my whole life. My lady guide walked me to a room that had a large screen in it. On the screen, I saw two forms of Light conjoining with one another in the act of making Love. My guide then asked me to tell her which was the male and which was the female? I said, "I dunno!" She smiled at me and said it does not matter. She went on to say that the two Lights were what God saw when he looked upon us. She explained that God always sees us as our higher selves and that gender is a very temporary thing that will not be around forever. It was further explained to me that God himself is both a Mother essence and a Father essence to us, therefore; God fully understands our attractions for members of similar genders. It was told to me (or rather I was reminded) that there are no mistakes in the way each of us were made. God knew what each of us would be challenged and blessed with. We each act according to our heart (or developed Soul center) and as we mature Spiritually, we come up higher each time.

One other thing I was shown was a couple engaging in activities that focused on Lust rather than Love. My lady guide said that these individuals were in great spiritual duress and bringing upon themselves a life that would present much challenge. I saw that their Soul Lights began to dim significantly and there was a dark haze all about them. My lady guide then told me a time would come when these individuals would need to learn to come to God with their sexual selves, so that he could help them to use their sexuality in a more Loving way. More than likely, emotional or mental illness would emerge and help guide them to a more Loving path of expression. As I looked upon the figures, I sadly commented that lust was a major factor that involved many gay people. The lady smiled at me and explained that all fall into lust before we fully embrace the Light within ourselves. Later the lady also revealed to me that the two dimly beings in spiritual duress ... had been a married heterosexual couple.

154 *Liz Dale, Ph.D. and Kevin Williams*

WHAT WAS THE DARK HAZE?

The dark haze was what I call gray or shadow energy. This is a challenging type of essence that coexists with us on the planet. I believe this is what the Bible refers to as demons. These entities' job unto Creation is to help bring us additional weight and life obstacles which match our non-positive or unloving thoughts. With the weight of their essence on us, our inner Light is blocked. After a period of time where we go stumbling around in the darkness of our lives, we are once again encouraged to return to more Loving thought and action. As soon as we produce enough Light in our Soul from having been Loving, the gray or shadow energy is then popped off of us. **WHERE THERE IS LIGHT, DARKNESS CANNOT REMAIN!** However, we must maintain Loving action and thinking because if we return to a less positive way of being, these entities return bringing reinforcements with them. When this happens it is time to do spiritual warfare!

HOW DOES ONE DO SPIRITUAL WARFARE?

My answer might surprise you. Spiritual warfare is a practice of celebration. Why? Because celebration is the very opposite to depression which is what dark energies want us to fall into so they can tighten their grip on us.

Dark energies do not want us to celebrate and rejoice in the fact that beyond any truth … God is Love and God's Love has already won and achieved victory over any challenge that might come against us. It is up to us to open ourselves up and receive God's Love … All we must do is simply … believe!

The dark forces of challenging energy come to steal our Joy! The reason for this is because misery Loves company! Ever notice that?

People who are in the habit of being down adore it when others come and join them in their destructive pity party. Well, these "sad parties" are for the most part attended by darkened energies. Because dark energy is joyless, it wants us to become the same! However, never forget … the Joy of the Lord is our Strength!

When you feel as if you are being overcome by shadow … it is time for you to announce "NO MORE!" and celebrate your life! I highly recommend that during times when you feel something evil is trying to sneak up on you from the back door, swing open the front door and let the Light of God's Love come in your life in every way you can think of or Holy Spirit shows you. Throw out all behaviors you know to be destructive and unpositive. Allow no negative conversation to come from your mouth! Only affirm the positive!

Hint: Turn off the TV... and put on the CD player! Use music to heal your life! Keep in mind that when we go back home to Heaven, music is what God uses to restore our Souls! Powerful and stirring music is everywhere! If we are wise, we will play good Love affirming music in our environments often! I use everything from Gospel to Enya. Play that wonderful music in your homes, cars and work spaces everyday. Think of it as a can of Lysol that not only helps to disinfect your space from dark energy, it spreads colorful rainbow Light for you to walk into.

SOMETIMES I FEEL SO ASHAMED BECAUSE OF MY WEAKNESSES!

Never allow shame to come down on you because you have fallen into challenge. Every person on this planet has to endure this process and every person has been made stronger because of it. The occurrence of challenge is a part of God's perfect plan. Most think that they have to make themselves perfect before God will have anything to do with them. This is not so. It is our challenges in life that help us to find him! Once we get past our challenges, we understand the great unconditional Love he has for us and he uses our experiences to help dislodge others who are stuck in the same places we have been.

WHAT HAPPENS TO ME SPIRITUALLY ONCE I AM ABLE TO HAVE VICTORY OVER A CHALLENGE?

Each time we are able to build our Light back up, we then add solid muscle to our Souls. I am speaking of spiritual muscle (made of dense Light) which will help us to lift up issues and challenges that might have been impossible to get through before. It is through this method that God prepares us to undertake our life's mission. This is why many people have difficult lives before they come into their glory. The challenges they faced will have strengthened them to the degree that once they arrive at their Divine destination, very little will be able to shake them.

WHAT IS EGO?

Ego is that thing that helps us learn what LOVE is by showing us what it is not. All things on Earth must come to a place of balance. All things must have a parallel. This is how we are each caused to grow Spiritually. Just as a face (due to gravity) may wrinkle with time, so does a Soul become weighed down with ego. Ego is always LOVE'S opposite. Love raises vibration and ego lowers it. Ego is a mental essence that each of us is made to endure for as long as we walk the planet. Ego is that thing that tells us in our mind, "No you can't do that ... because you're not talented, thin, good-looking, wealthy, intelligent, young, strong, interesting or intuitive ENOUGH!" This is the voice of the Liar. The Liar is the voice of ego. Let me put it this way: wherever there is separation, condemnation, self-doubt, lack-mentality, bitterness, hostility or segregation ... you can best be sure ego is not far behind.

WHY DOES EGO DO THIS?

Ego wants to keep you earthbound and Heavenless for as long as it can. It is an essence that has been sent here to learn just as you have. However, it has a duty to challenge each of us and cause us to learn as it learns for itself. There is nothing to fear about the ego. It is just a fragile, spoiled child that screams and rants until it gets what it wants. And like any child, if you ignore it during its temper flare long enough, sooner or later it will get the message that those kinds of methods are not productive and will not yield positive results.

WHAT ABOUT THE DEVIL?

If you understand the ego, you will understand the concept of the devil. Satanic frequency is the LOW-RANGE frequency that surrounds us in our collective thinking. It is the opposite of the HIGH, INCOMPREHENSIBLE LOVING frequency of God. Please hear me out on something...be careful of the music you listen to, the movies or TV you watch, the gossip or negative speaking you participate in. All these things LOWER the Soul's vibration. Lower vibration brings depression, disillusionment, disease and despair. The lower our Soul's vibration falls, the more these dark things come upon us. Once you fall into LOWER vibration, immediately seek to amend it with LOVING, HIGHER VIBRATIONAL THOUGHT. It is like anything else, the more you put into something, that is what the end result will be.

WHAT ABOUT HELL?

There is a place called "the Death Shadowed Valley," where some Souls may choose to go to if they feel too afraid, guilty or shameful to approach Heaven or God. This is an in-between place or dimension that separates Souls from this world and the next. ...And as I have discussed before ... being caught in this type of situation is a very difficult process to endure and can cause problems for both the living and the dead. However each of us has the ability to call out to God or to Christ ... and immediately ... we will be taken home to Heaven. Or we (the living) can pray and call out to God to send his Angels to come and take others home. It is important for us to understand that we each send ourselves to the places our Soul believes it most belongs. We do that now here on planet Earth. Those stuck in addiction, lust, bitterness and hate -- these are the ones truly in hell. But the moment we choose Love, we can get ourselves out. God never sends us anywhere we do not wish to stay. We have totally misunderstood the concept of hell on this planet.

WHAT ABOUT A PLACE OF BURNING FIRE?

I do know of a place in the deep regions of the Realm where I saw great caverns of electrical blue fire. However, I understood that this place was for the purpose of Loving purification. God would never send his precious creatures to a place to be burned or harmed. It is completely contrary to our Creator's nature.

Life is full of hellish experiences and God would prefer we keep ourselves from as many of these things as possible, so that we do not overly darken our Souls ... which in time will only keep us from remembering who we really are.

WHAT ARE SOME THINGS I SHOULD WATCH OUT FOR?

Never allow hatred to exist within you! Do all you can to remove it from your life. Hatred is the greatest toxin known to humankind. Never allow yourself to remain angry. Anger brings disease and challenging energy. Do all you can to avoid excess. Excessive food, drink, lust, intoxicants, ambitious planning, competition, and (of course) grief, bitterness, resentment and judgment. The gray energies can easily fool us into becoming unbalanced if we over indulge in any one person, place, thought or thing. Be sure to get plenty of fresh air, exercise, rest and watch what poisons (unnatural substances) you put into your body. Drink plenty of water. Your spirit wants to help you wash toxins out of your body. Water was made for this purpose. Your body is the temple for the Spirit. The ego will do all it can to have you disrespect yourself so that you might ultimately lose your sense of importance and Divine worth. Beware of the ego at all times and look for it in all situations and people. Once you spot ego, ask God to help you assume spiritual control. Never be ashamed to ask for God's help. He is right there waiting to show you the way out of your dilemma. Seek to be respectful to all living creatures. Be generous whenever you can. Remember that Mother Earth has been a gracious host, let us do all we can to keep her a wonderful place for our children to live.

HOW DID YOUR NEAR-DEATH EXPERIENCE AFFECT YOUR MUSIC CAREER?

When I came back from my NDE, I made a promise to myself that I would only record and sing songs that had a positive and healing influence on the Soul. So far, I have kept that promise and I'm honored to hear from those who tell me they play my music in their homes, cars, at work and in their healing spaces every day or at least several times a week. It pleases me greatly to hear from these folks and then find out that the music is helping them to heal from trauma, break spells of depression ... or motivate and cause positive momentum in their lives!

Music filled with strong flowing melodic lines, lush tones and positive lyrics can cause us to become filled with Light thus enhancing our ability to give and receive Love. Because God is actually part MUSIC, good positive music can greatly help us maintain a sense of connection and union with our eternal Spirit.

After my NDE, I came back fully understanding the power music has over our lives; as God gifted me with an ability to be sensitive to tones held within the music. Now I have an advanced capacity to comprehend what tones are secretly communicating to the Soul. I use this ability when I write, arrange and produce mine (and other's) music. In fact, that is why I typically write the melody first and then put the words down later. For me, music is a message waiting for a translation. An artist is a person whom God has blessed with a tremendous emotional vocabulary to communicate to others (who are still developing their impressions about the world that surrounds them.)

In my NDE, I learned that dark tones and harshly/suggestively sung music (with negative lyrics) listened to over time, makes our mind and Soul progressively distressed and dysfunctional. Usually the artists doing these kinds of songs are typically distressed and dysfunctional themselves. It is because of this that I strongly advise people who are working on fixing their lives or staying on a Light filled path, to stay as far away from such music as much as possible! Unfortunately, much of the "popular music" in today's culture is littered with destructive lyrics and non-nurturing tones. Without being aware, the general public has been trained by the greed based media to actually become entertained by dysfunctional songs, and most people (especially youth) have no clue that much of the music (they are listening to) is actually injuring them emotionally! Some may have an inkling of this fact, but because of media hypnotism, socialized peer pressure, boredom or lack of quality music ... they listen anyway. And we wonder why we have so much violence, materialism, uncontrolled lust and other issues? From what I now understand spiritually, the TV and the radio has just about done modern day culture in! And if we don't start becoming more observant to the negative programming we are filling our minds with day after day, we are going to be caused to become numb to what is actually good for us and not be able to make effectual and lasting "positive" momentum in our lives! We have to train ourselves to pay close attention to how the music we are listening to makes us feel. Does it make us feel peaceful, joyous or dynamic? Or does it leave us feeling aggressive, resentful, bitter, lustful or arrogant? Be careful! Music is powerful stuff. It can either help heal you or hurt you. With all my Heart I advise you to listen wisely!

WHAT WOULD BE THE MOST IMPORTANT THING YOU COULD SAY NOW?

Please never forget ... You are so Loved! Never is there a time where you are unseen or forgotten! To know Love ... you must practice Loving! Remember, your challenges in life are here as gifts ... once you succeed in getting past them, you will be rewarded by being filled with Loving and healing Light. There is no greater feeling than this. When in doubt, remember -- Love is always the answer!

God bless you my precious brothers and sisters! Please know I am sending out Love and good energy to whomever will receive it!

Be Loving to one another and Love will be good to you.

17

CONCLUSION

Many years ago, visiting my first IANDS conference – Oakland, CA – in 1996, I heard a plenary speaker mention that she didn't know what the GAY NDE would look like. I investigated further and realized the LGBT (Lesbian – Gay – Bisexual – Transgender) NDE research had never been done. So I took this project on and asked any LGBT near-death experiencers to write up their experience. By 2001, the *Crossing Over and Coming Home* book came out in which NDErs from numerous walks of life sent in their stories to share with others. The book was generally well received and the material was presented at a number of IANDS conferences over the years. By 2007, I put the book on Amazon and Kindle when it was possible to do so. Over time it was obvious that5 this LGBT near-death experience would be more scientifically and statistically useful if our group was compared to Non-Gay NDErs. This is how this book came about.

Thanks to Kevin Williams (webmaster of www.near-death.com), the second study of cross cultural comparison from LGBT and Non-Gay

NDEr was set up. Many NDErs were interested and sent in their NDEs anonymously sharing in their journeys for others to read.

Over the past few years, Kevin and I have worked to see this project through. Now that this project's results are finally about to be published, it is important to talk about the final conclusion. The two groups of LGBT and Non-Gay NDEs have shown *no significant differences* on all areas of inquiry. The part I want to add to this has to do with LGBT people in general. All over the world LGBT people have been unfairly treated, persecuted, discriminated against and yet it is very clear that on the Other Side there is no such persecution. All of us are treated with love / concern / care / appreciation by those who we meet once beginning the journey through the Thin Veil. The freedom and love that we all receive is clearly felt by all of us who have had NDEs. Any cross cultural comparison should show the same thing. This is a great relief from what we have experienced while living "on this side" and having much to deal with while on the earthly side awaiting great changes which are yet to come.

BIBLIOGRAPHY

Atwater, P.M.H. Aftereffects of Near-Death States. Retrieved from IANDS website, https://iands.org/ndes/about-ndes/common-aftereffects.html, 2017.

Auster, Paul. I Thought My Father Was God and Other True Tales From NPR's National Story Project. Henry Holt and Co, 2001.

Berman, Phillip. The Journey Home. Gallery Books, 1998.

"Bisexuality", retrieved from Wikipedia, https://en.wikipedia.org/wiki/Bisexuality.

Bush, Nancy Evans. "Distressing Near-Death Experience." Retrieved from https://psi-encyclopedia.spr.ac.uk/articles/distressing-near-death-experience, 2022.

Dale, Liz. Crossing Over and Coming Home. Kindle Edition. Amazon Kindle Direct Publishing, 2017.
https://www.amazon.com/dp/B078QJGHSH/

Dale, Liz. Crossing Over and Coming Home. Papertback Edition. Amazon Kindle Direct Publishing, 2017. https://www.amazon.com/dp/ 197935040X/

Diamond, Debra. Life After Near Death: Miraculous Stories of Healing and Transformation in the Extraordinary Lives of People With Newfound Powers. Weiser Publishing, 2016.

"Gay", retrieved from Wikipedia, https://en.wikipedia.org/wiki/Gay.

Greyson, B. & Bush, N. E. "Distressing near-death experiences" in Bailey, L. W. & Yates, J. (Eds.) (1996). The Near-Death Experience: A Reader. New York: Routledge.

Greyson, B. & Ring, K. "The Life Changes Inventory - Revised", Journal of Near-Death Studies, 23(1), Fall 2004.

"Intelligence quotient", retrieved from Wikipedia, https://en.wikipedia.org/wiki/Intelligence_quotient.

"Lesbian", retrieved from Wikipedia, https://en.wikipedia.org/wiki/Lesbian.

"LGBT", retrieved from Wikipedia, https://en.wikipedia.org/wiki/LGBT.

Long, Jeffrey. Carmel Bell's Near-Death Experience. Retrieved from https://www.nderf.org/Experiences/1carmel_b_nde.html.

Lundahl, Craig. "Lessons From Near-Death Experiences For Humanity", Journal of Near-Death Studies, 12(1), Fall 1993.

Martin, Laurelynn. Searching for Home: A Personal Journey of Transformation and Healing After a Near-Death Experience. Cosmic Concepts Press. 1996.

Moody, Raymond. Life After Life. Mockingbird Books, 1976.

"Non-Gay", from Oxford Dictionary,
https://www.lexico.com/en/definition/non-gay.

Oakford, David. Soul Bared: A Metaphysical Journey. Independently published, 2018.

"Outline of parapsychology", retrieved from Wikipedia,
https://en.wikipedia.org/wiki/Outline_of_parapsychology.

"Personality", retrieved from Wikipedia,
https://en.wikipedia.org/wiki/Personality.

"Personality changes", retrieved from Wikipedia,
https://en.wikipedia.org/wiki/Personality_changes.

"Queer", retrieved from Wikipedia,
https://en.wikipedia.org/wiki/Queer.

"Questioning (sexuality and gender)", retrieved from Wikipedia, https://
en.wikipedia.org/wiki/Questioning_(sexuality_and_gender).

Ring, Kenneth. Heading Toward Omega: In Search of the Meaning of the Near-Death Experience. Harper Perennial. 1985.

Ring, Kenneth. Lessons From The Light: What We Can Learn from the Near-Death Experience. Moment Point Press. 2006.

Rommer, Barbara. Blessing in Disguise: Another Side of the Near-Death Experience. Llewellyn Publications, 2000.

San Filippo, David. Religious Interpretations of Near-Death Experiences, Retrieved from https://near-death.com/religious-interpretations/.

"Sexuality and gender identity-based cultures", retrieved from Wikipedia, https://en.wikipedia.org/wiki/Sexuality_and_gender_identity-based_cultures.

Speranza, Mindy. Visit to Heaven: What I Learned on the Other Side. CreateSpace Publishing. 2016.

"Transgender", retrieved from Wikipedia, https://en.wikipedia.org/wiki/Transgender.

Williams, Kevin. Beverly Brodsky's Near-Death Experience. Retrieved from https://near-death.com/beverly-brodsky/.

Williams, Kevin. Christian Andreason's Near-Death Experience. Retrieved from https://near-death.com/christian-andreason-nde/.

Williams, Kevin. David Oakford's Near-Death Experience. Retrieved from https://near-death.com/david-oakford/.

Williams, Kevin. Donna Gatti's Near-Death Experience. Retrieved from https://near-death.com/donna-gatti/.

Williams, Kevin. Laurelynn Martin's Near-Death Experience. Retrieved from https://near-death.com/laurelynn-martin/.

Williams, Kevin. Martha St. Claire's Near-Death Experience. Retrieved from https://near-death.com/martha-st-claire/.

Williams, Kevin. The Trigger of Hypnosis: Palden Jenkin's Near-Death Experience. Retrieved from https://near-death.com/trigger-of-hypnosis/.

About The Authors

Liz Dale, Ph.D. (www.lizdale.org) is a clinical psychologist whose expertise is near-death experience (NDE) research within the LGBT community. Upon looking for literature dealing with NDEs in the gay community, Dr. Dale found that no studies existed. So she contacted the LGBT community through a popular local newspaper asking for participants who would rise to the challenge of being among the first individuals to participate in such a study. In the fall of 1997, her IANDS support group began face-to-face discussions of their NDEs with some group members having never shared their experiences before. After over a two-year period looking for participants, more than thirty people came forward with their stories. Her support group decided to publish these amazing stories and her study their NDEs — the first study of NDEs in the LGBT community. Dr. Dale published her findings in her book entitled, "Crossing Over and Coming Home: Twenty-One Authors Discuss the Gay Near-Death Experience as Spiritual Transformation" (Emerald Ink Publications, 2000).

Kevin R. Williams (www.near-death.com) is a computer programmer with a Bachelor of Science degree in Computer Science. He is the webmaster of the website "Near-Death Experiences and the Afterlife." The website is one the most comprehensive website on the internet about near-death experiences. He is an active member of IANDS, the International Association for Near-Death Studies. Williams currently lives near Sacramento, California, where he continues to write and maintain his website.

Printed in the United States
by Baker & Taylor Publisher Services